All Rise

Dignity is not negotiable.

—Vartan Gregorian

ALL RISE

Somebodies, Nobodies, and the Politics of Dignity

Robert W. Fuller

Berrett-Koehler Publishers, Inc.
235 Montgomery Street, Suite 650
San Francisco, CA 94104-2916
Tel: (415) 288-0260   Fax: (415) 362-2512   www.bkconnection.com

Ordering Information
Quantity sales. Special discounts are available on quantity purchases by corporations, associations, and others. For details, contact the "Special Sales Department" at the Berrett-Koehler address above.
Individual sales. Berrett-Koehler publications are available through most bookstores. They can also be ordered direct from Berrett-Koehler: Tel: (800) 929-2929; Fax: (802) 864-7626; www.bkconnection.com
Orders for college textbook/course adoption use. Please contact Berrett-Koehler: Tel: (800) 929-2929; Fax: (802) 864-7626.
Orders by U.S. trade bookstores and wholesalers. Please contact Publishers Group West, 1700 Fourth Street, Berkeley, CA 94710. Tel: (510) 528-1444; Fax (510) 528-3444.

Berrett-Koehler and the BK logo are registered trademarks of Berrett-Koehler Publishers, Inc.

Printed in the United States of America

Berrett-Koehler books are printed on long-lasting acid-free paper. When it is available, we choose paper that has been manufactured by environmentally responsible processes. These may include using trees grown in sustainable forests, incorporating recycled paper, minimizing chlorine in bleaching, or recycling the energy produced at the paper mill.

Library of Congress Cataloging-in-Publication Data
Fuller, Robert W. (Robert Works), 1936–
    All rise : somebodies, nobodies, and the politics of dignity / Robert W. Fuller.
       p. cm.
    Includes index.
    ISBN-10: 1-57675-385-9; ISBN-13: 978-1-57675-385-9
1. Social classes. 2. Social values. I. Title.

    HT609.F815 2006
    305.5—dc22

                                                                    2005055591

First Edition
12 11 10 09 08 07 06   10 9 8 7 6 5 4 3 2 1

Copyeditor: Sandra Beris   Proofreader: Henrietta Bensussen
Interior Designer: Gopa & Ted2, Books & Design   Indexer: Medea Minnich
Production: Linda Jupiter, Jupiter Productions

To Claire Sheridan

CONTENTS

INTRODUCTION
WHAT IS RANKISM?

WHY DO YOU SMILE? CHANGE BUT THE NAME, AND
IT IS OF YOURSELF THAT THE TALE IS TOLD.
— HORACE, ROMAN POET AND SATIRIST

A Once and Future Nobody

NONE OF US likes to be taken for a nobody. In order to protect our dignity, we cultivate the skill of presenting ourselves as a somebody. But despite our best efforts, it may come to pass that we wake up one morning and find ourselves in Nobodyland.

At midlife that happened to me, and for quite some time I couldn't seem to get out. Then one morning I heard new words to an old slogan buzzing in my head: "Nobodies of the world, unite! We have nothing to lose but our shame."

A slogan like that calls for a manifesto. In a few frenzied months I wrote a first draft, which I called *The Nobody Book.* It argued that nobodies are not defenseless against the put-downs of somebodies and showed what they can do in response to such attacks.

I made a half-dozen copies and foisted them on my friends. The first thing I heard from them was, "Change the title! No one would want to read something called *The Fat Book* and no one will want to read *The Nobody Book* either." But everyone insisted on telling me about the times they'd been "nobodied." I started collecting their stories and recalled a few of my own.

I remembered Arlene in second grade, exiled to the hall as punishment for having dirty fingernails. I winced at the memory of Burt, who had bullied me and my friends at summer camp. I recalled with chagrin how my playmates and I had tormented a kid with Down syndrome, and how Professor Mordeau had made fun of my faulty French accent. Memories of the Sunday school teacher who threatened us with eternal damnation returned.

I began to see stories of humiliation and indignity in the news as well as close at hand: abuse scandals in churches and prisons, corporations defaulting on employee pensions, hypercompetitive parents berating child athletes, the staff at my parents' retirement home patronizing residents.

The Abuse of Rank

One day all these behaviors came into a single focus: they could all be seen as abuses of rank—more precisely, the power attached to rank. I recognized myself as a once and future nobody, and wondered if that wasn't everyone's fate. As the anecdotes multiplied, I incorporated them into the manuscript. After numerous reorganizations of the material, I printed a dozen copies, passed them around and awaited the verdict. People still hedged their bets, but they all wanted me to hear about their own attempts to get out of Nobodyland.

The reframing and rewriting continued. A third draft. The analysis was extended and gained in clarity. A fourth. After a few years, I submitted a version to several publishers. They responded with boilerplate rejections. One editor opined that the material was compelling and might even have broad appeal, but saw an insurmountable problem: "Nobodies don't buy books!"

A friend suggested creating a Web site where I could at least give the book away. So I hired a college math major to design one. Her creation gave oxygen to the project. We dubbed the site breakingranks.net, and it's still going strong on the Web.

Overnight, it got thousands of hits. On an online forum, strangers shared their stories of abuse and discrimination. Two thousand visitors to the site downloaded the free manuscript. One of them put a copy into the hands of a small publisher, and just when I'd about given up hope of ever seeing it appear between two covers I received an e-mail inquiring about rights to it. A meeting was arranged, a contract signed, and in the spring of 2003 New Society Publishers in British Columbia brought out a hardcover edition of *Somebodies and Nobodies: Overcoming the Abuse of Rank.*[1]

Getting the word out that spring was made more difficult by the Iraq war, the start of which coincided to the day with the book's publication. Round-the-clock coverage of the conflict lasted about a month, but during the blackout I got a break: Oprah's magazine featured the book in an article titled "R-E-S-P-E-C-T," and suddenly my phone started ringing.[2] Twelve cities and a hundred interviews later, the book had found its audience. For a few heady days, it even managed to edge out the latest Harry Potter book at Amazon.com. It seems that nobodies do buy books after all!

Recognizing Rankism

Nobodyland isn't really such a bad place, so long as you aren't trying to get out. You can do a lot of good work there, and since you're out of sight, you are free to make mistakes, explore new ideas, and develop them until you're ready to try them in public. When, at long last, I did get the chance to do so, I got an earful in response.

Some people scolded me for wasting their time: "Everything in your book is in the Bible. It shouldn't take 150 pages to get to the golden rule." A couple of wary souls feared this was another cult. And a handful protested, "Not another 'ism'!" and dismissed the idea of *rankism* as "just more political correctness," "radical egalitarianism," or "Fabian drivel."

But most respondents—even the self-confessed cynics—welcomed the naming and spotlighting of rank-based abuse and expressed the hope that by targeting rankism we could consolidate our gains over the now-familiar isms—racism, sexism, ageism, ableism,[3] and so on—and eventually extend the sway of democratic principles so as to secure dignity for everybody. Here are a few remarks posted on the Web site or sent as e-mail:

> Rankism is the ism that, once eradicated, would pretty much eliminate the rest of them.

> Rankism is so ingrained, so common, that it's hard to even notice it.

> Rankism gives a name to something we've all experienced but probably not given much thought to. Once you have a name for it, you see it everywhere.

> It's comforting to know that a lot of the insults I've put up with in my life are being experienced by people everywhere. I for one am sick of being nobodied.

> Recognizing rankism makes you more conscious of your dignity.

> I have begun using the term rankism, explained it to my friends, and now they are using it, too.

In the three years following the publication of *Somebodies and Nobodies* I learned that there is indeed an iceberg of indignation out there of which we're seeing only the tip. Below the waterline lies the bottled-up resentments of millions who are nobodied every day. I heard from kids, parents, teachers, nurses, physicians, managers, professionals, and workers of every stripe. The impotent rage they must contain—whether at home, in school, or on the job—exacts a toll on their health and happiness and hence on their creativity and productivity. Occasionally their repressed indignation erupts in what others see as a senseless act of violence. But violence is rarely, if ever, senseless. If it seems so, we've simply failed to understand it. Like the original n-word, *nobody* is an epithet that packs a powerful punch. That is why we're so desperate to pass as somebodies and shield ourselves from rankism's punishing sting.

Another thing I've learned is that once people have a diagnosis for what ails them, they want a cure for it. Many asked me for more concrete strategies for fighting rankism. They also wanted a clearer picture of what a *dignitarian* society—a society in which rank-holders are held accountable, rankism is disallowed, and dignity is broadly protected—would look like and tools that could be used for building one. The purpose of this book is to address those requests.

For those of you who haven't read *Somebodies and Nobodies,* here's a little background.

Power Matters

Like most people who experienced the social movements of the sixties, my attention at the time was drawn to personal attributes such as color, gender, disability, or age, each of which was associated with its own form of prejudice. But as a college president in the early seventies, I found myself dealing with the women's, black, and student movements all at once and from a position of authority at the vortex of the storms they were generating on campus. This gave me a vantage point from which I began to sense that something more than trait-sanctioned discrimination was going on, something deeper and more encompassing. What struck me was that, despite changes in the cast of characters and differences in rhetoric, each of these movements could be seen as a group of weaker and more vulnerable "nobodies" petitioning for an end to oppression and indignity at the hands of entrenched, more powerful "somebodies."

From this point of view, it becomes obvious that characteristics such as religion, color, gender, and age are merely excuses for discrimination, never its cause. Indeed, such features signify weakness only when there is a social consensus in place that handicaps those bearing them. Anti-Semitism, Jim Crow segregation, patriarchy, and homophobia are all complex social agreements that have functioned to disempower whole categories of people and keep them susceptible to abuse and exploitation.

The personal traits that define the various identity groups are pretexts around which social stratifications are built and maintained. But at the deepest level, these arrangements foster and support injustice based on something less conspicuous but no less profound in its consequences: rank in the social hierarchy. All the various, seemingly disparate forms of discrimination actually have one common root: the presumption and assertion of rank to the detriment of others.

Providing further evidence for this shift in perspective was my realization that just as some whites bully other whites, so also do some blacks exploit other blacks and some women demean other women. Clearly, such intraracial and intragender abuses can't easily be accounted for within the usual trait-centered analyses. One approach is to account for black-on-black prejudice—sometimes called *colorism*—in terms of the "internalization of white oppression." But this explains one malady (black racism) in terms of another (white racism) and brings us no closer to a remedy for either. If the goal is to end racism of all kinds, it's more fruitful to see both inter- and intraracial discrimination as based on differences in power—that is, on who holds the higher position in a particular setting and therefore commands an advantage that forces victims to submit to their authority.

Viewing things in terms of power instead of color, gender, and so on is not intended to divorce the dynamics of racial or other forms of prejudice from the specific justifications that particular groups of somebodies use to buttress their claims to supremacy. But it does direct our attention to the real source of ongoing domination—a power advantage—and suggests that we'll end social subordination of every kind only as we disallow abuse stemming from simply having high enough rank to get away with it.

As the implications of all this sank in I realized that, as with the familiar liberation causes, abuse of the power associated with rank could not be effectively addressed so long as there was no name for it. Absent one, nobodies were in a position similar to that of women before the term *sexism* was coined. Writing in 1963, Betty Friedan characterized the plight of women as "the problem that has no name."[4] By 1968, the problem had acquired one: sexism. That simple word intensified consciousness-raising and debate and provided a rallying cry for a movement to oppose power abuse linked to gender.

A similar dynamic has played out with other identity groups seeking redress of their grievances. Those discriminated against on the basis of their race unified against racism. The elderly targeted *ageism.* By analogy, I adopted the term *rankism* to describe abuses of power associated with rank.

The coinage rankism is related to the colloquialisms *pulling rank* and *ranking on* someone, both of which bear witness to the signal importance of rank in human interactions. It is also worth noting that as an adjective, rank means foul, fetid, or smelly, and the verb *to rankle* means to cause resentment or bitterness. Although there is no etymological relationship between these usages and the word *rank* in the sense of position in a hierarchy, it's fitting that the word *rankism* picks up by association the malodor of its sound-alikes.

Rank can refer to either rank in society generally (social rank) or rank in a more narrowly defined context (such as within an institution or family). Thus, rankism occurs not just between and within social identity groups but in schools, businesses, health care organizations, religious institutions, the military, and government bureaucracies as well. Indeed, since most organizations are hierarchical and hierarchies are built around gradations of power, it comes as no surprise that they are breeding grounds for rank-based abuse.

Examples from everyday life include a boss harassing an employee, a doctor demeaning a nurse, a professor exploiting a graduate student, and students bullying each other. On a societal scale are headline-making stories of political and corporate corruption, sexual abuse by members of the clergy, and the maltreatment of elders in nursing homes.

Photos of the humiliation of Iraqi prisoners by their guards gave the entire world a look at rankism's arrogant face. Hurricane Katrina made visible its most common victims. The wealthy and connected, even those of moderate means, got out of New Orleans ahead of time. The poor, the sick, prisoners, the old, and those lacking transportation were trapped by nature's fury and then left to cope on their own during days of inaction by government officials and agencies. The inadequacies of the initial government response have since been compounded by another, deeply ingrained form of rankism—the regionalism that, since the Civil War, has manifested as the North holding itself superior to the South.

In addition to its universality, rankism differs from the familiar trait-based abuses because rank is not fixed the way race and gender generally are, but rather changes depending on the context. Someone can hold high rank in one setting (for example, at home) and simultaneously be low on the totem pole in another (at work). Likewise, we can feel powerful at one time and powerless at another, as when we move from childhood to adulthood and then from our "prime" into old age, or when we experience the loss of a job, a partner, or our health. As a result, most of us have been both victims and perpetrators of discrimination based on rank.

In summary, rankism occurs when those with authority use the power of their position to secure unwarranted advantages or benefits for themselves at the expense of others. It is the illegitimate use of rank, and equally, the use of rank illegitimately acquired or held. The familiar isms are all examples of the latter form. They are based on the construction and maintenance of differences in social rank that violate constitutional guarantees of equal protection under the law.

The relationship between rankism and the specific isms targeted by identity politics can be compared to that between cancer and its subspecies. For centuries the group of diseases that are now all seen as varieties of cancer were regarded as distinct illnesses. No one realized that lung, breast, and other organ-specific cancers all had their origins in a similar kind of cellular malfunction. In this metaphor, racism, sexism, homophobia, and other varieties of prejudice are analogous to organ-specific cancers and rankism is the blanket malady analogous to cancer itself. The familiar isms are subspecies of rankism. Just as medicine is now exploring grand strategies that will be applicable to all kinds of cancer, so too it may be more effective at this point to raise our sights and attack rankism itself rather than focusing on its individual varieties one by one.

Another analogy is to waves in water. You can look at racism, ageism, classism, homophobia, and so on as waves, or you can focus on the water of rankism. Neither perspective makes the other an optical illusion.[5]

Presently, backlash threatens the hard-won gains of the firmly established civil rights and women's movements as well as the more nascent ones such as the movement for people with disabilities or the GLBT (gay, lesbian, bisexual, and transgender) movement. Moreover, identity politics generally is running into diminishing returns. Could it be that to complete the eradication of the familiar isms, we will have to include everyone—somebodies and nobodies alike—and redirect our attack onto the rankism that afflicts us all?

The Dignitarian Perspective

I almost never make it through an interview or a talk without being asked, "Are you proposing that we do away with rank?" It is crucial to understand that rank itself is not necessarily a problem. Unless rank is inherently illegitimate—as are, for example, the social rankings that have made second-class citizens of various identity groups—then the problem is not with rank per se but rather with the abuse of rank. This distinction goes to the heart of many of the most vexing issues that arise in our personal lives, society, and national politics.

The confusion occurs because rank is so commonly misused that many people mistakenly conclude that the only remedy is to abolish it. This makes no more sense than attempting to solve racial problems by doing away with all races but one, or addressing gender issues by eliminating one gender. Ignoring differences in aptitude, ability, and performance and attempting to eradicate the differences of rank that reflect them has repeatedly failed those who have tried it. The socialists of nineteenth-century Europe and the communists of the twentieth century disappointed their supporters. And when egalitarian ideologies did prevail, those leaderships typically imposed even worse tyrannies than the ones they replaced.

Abolishing distinctions of rank that facilitate cooperation can also weaken a society to the point that it becomes vulnerable to existing enemies or invites new ones. History suggests that political and social models that try to do away with rank altogether are naïvely utopian and that societies that adopt them court catastrophe. The nineteenth-century French historian Alexis de Tocqueville devoted a chapter of his classic *Democracy in America* to the connections between equality and despotism.[6]

When legitimately earned and properly used, rank is an important—often indispensable—organizational tool for accomplishing group goals. The more central rank is to achieving an organization's mission—for example, in the military—the more critical it is to distinguish it from rankism and to honor the former while eliminating the latter. Not every assertion of rank is rankist—only those that put the dignity of the high-ranking above that of those they serve.

We rightfully admire and love authorities—parents, teachers, bosses, political leaders—who hold their rank and use the power that comes with it in an exemplary way. Accepting their leadership entails no loss of self-respect or opportunity on the part of subordinates. It is when people abuse their power to demean or disadvantage those they outrank that seeds of indignity are sown. Over time, indignity turns to indignation, and smarting victims may be left thirsting for vengeance. The consequences can range from relatively benign foot-dragging all the way to genocide.

Organization of this Book

Somebodies and Nobodies concluded with a vision of a dignitarian society. Such a society does not aim to abolish or equalize ranks, but rather holds that regardless of our rank, we are all equal when it comes to dignity. The word *dignitarian* is introduced to set this model apart from utopian egalitarian ones. The dignitarian approach sees the establishment of equal dignity as a stepping-stone to the more fair, just, and tolerant societies that political thinkers have long envisioned.[7]

This presents a chicken-and-egg problem: In building a dignity movement to overcome rankism, what should be the first objective—cultural or institutional change? In other words, should we focus on eradicating the rankism within ourselves and our culture or target the rankism "out there" in organizations and society? Some hold that we can't change our institutions until we change our personal attitudes; others insist that the institutions must be changed first because only then are the people affected by them at liberty to change.

The argument is unproductive. Certain people are drawn to personal psychology and cultural values, while others focus on reforming institutional policy or electoral politics. An advance on either flank makes possible an advance on the other.

Although the dynamics of social transformation are nonlinear, exposition is not. A writer has to choose an order in which to present ideas. The first three chapters of this book lay the groundwork by sketching the scope and impact of rankism, envisioning a dignity movement to overcome it, and introducing a key tool we'll use along the way: model building. The notion of model building may at first sound technical, perhaps even esoteric. But the use of this instrument is not limited to scientists and philosophers; on the contrary, as we'll see, it's commonplace in social situations as well.

Once we have this tool in our repertoire, we'll apply it first to explore how we can reshape our primary social and civic institutions so they become dignitarian. Chapters 4 through 8 examine what workplaces, schools, health care organizations, the economy, and politics would look like if they embodied dignitarian values.

Next, we'll use modeling to better the odds of establishing ourselves as dignitarians. The concluding chapters 9 through 12 develop a philosophical perspective that supports a dignitarian world. The afterword gives suggestions on how to get started.

WHAT'S AT STAKE 1

RANKISM EXPLAINS A LOT OF THE BAD BEHAVIOR WE SEE IN BOTH INSTITU-
TIONS AND CULTURES, AS WELL AS BETWEEN INDIVIDUALS. . . . GIVING IT A
NAME EMPOWERS THOSE ON THE RECEIVING END TO FIGHT IT, OR AT LEAST
TO RESIST THE CORROSIVE EFFECT IT MAY HAVE ON THEIR OWN SOULS.
—ESTHER DYSON, EDITOR, *RELEASE 1.0*

Seeing Rankism Everywhere

A COMMON RESPONSE to the notion of rankism is the one I had myself
soon after I started using the word: I began seeing it everywhere. This
surprised me at first, but not long afterward I realized this was a consequence of having defined rankism so broadly—as the abuse of the
power attached to rank. It stands to reason that something defined this
way would show up wherever power was in play—and that's almost
everywhere. Once I accepted the ubiquity of rankism, another question
arose. Could a concept that lumped so many seemingly different phenomena together really be useful?

Despite such hesitations, I kept spotting new examples of rankism on
a daily basis. What's more, I felt as though I were seeing them through
new eyes. Abuses I was resigned to, having long taken them for granted,
suddenly began to appear open to challenge. It seemed possible that if
we became more adept at identifying the common impulse from which
these transgressions derive, we could recondition ourselves to forgo
such behaviors.

Humans have managed to impose categorical illegitimacy on murder, incest, cannibalism, racism, and sexism. Some dominating, predatory behaviors that were the norm for centuries have diminished over time. As the consensus shifts about what's acceptable, even the impulse to engage in certain behaviors dissipates. Why couldn't this work with those that cause indignity, I wondered. Our species is learning to forgo racism. Couldn't we broaden the prohibition to all the various forms of rankism? I began to imagine a society in which targeting the dignity of others is no longer condoned, a world in which it gradually disappears in the same way that one can now begin to imagine racism becoming a behavior that utterly lacks social support.

Recently I read in the *New York Times* about a schoolteacher in rural China accused of serially raping the fourth- and fifth-grade girls in his class. His pupils had dared not protest the absolute authority tradition-ally held by teachers. The situation reminded me of the unquestioning esteem in which, at least until the recent sex abuse scandals, priests in the United States were typically held by their parishioners. As the arti-cle put it, "Parents grant teachers carte blanche, even condoning beat-ings, while students are trained to honor and obey teachers, never challenge them. 'The absolute authority of teachers in schools is one of the reasons that teachers are so fearless in doing what they want,' said an expert on Chinese education."[1]

Of course, rape is already a crime in almost all societies. The point is not that seeing rape as a form of rankism reveals its criminality. Many kinds of power abuse have acquired particular names of their own—for example, cronyism, embezzlement, extortion, nepotism, blackmail, McCarthyism, anti-Semitism, and sexual harassment. What identify-ing them all as rankism does is put them in a new light and reveal their commonality. Having the word *rankism* at one's disposal is a bit like putting on X-ray glasses that help you see through the many kinds of power abuse to the wrongful assertions of rank that figure in them all.

Reframing the problem in this way also suggests a way out—namely, by adopting a variant of the strategy that's already working against race- and gender-based abuses. To overcome racism and sexism, the targets had to organize and then collectively oppose their tormentors with a commensurate, credible countervailing force.

There are obvious differences between a movement to overcome rankism in general and the identity-based movements. When it comes to the familiar varieties of discrimination, the victims and the victimizers are, for the most part, distinguishable and separate groups: black and white, female and male, gay and straight, and so on. The same thing that makes it easy to identify potential victims of these familiar isms—discernible characteristics like color and gender—facilitates the formation of a solidarity group to confront the perpetrators.

In contrast, the perpetrators and targets of rankism—the somebodies and the nobodies, respectively—do not fall neatly into distinct groups. As we've seen, most of us have played both roles, depending on time and place.

So the question is: Are we willing to forgo the potential advantages of exploiting weaker people in return for credible assurances that our own dignity will be secure should it ever come to pass that we find ourselves in their nobody shoes? To paraphrase the epigraph that appears at the beginning of this book, could we make dignity non-negotiable?

The following chapters aim to show that we can. Before getting on with it, however, it's important to get a clearer sense of just what's at stake in taking on rank-based abuse.

Lethal Consequences

That rankism underpins all the trait-based forms of discrimination already makes it a far-reaching phenomenon, one that extends well beyond the realm of hurt feelings and bruised egos to the more destructive consequences of repression and oppression. But most people will be surprised to learn that there are many other ways—some of them quite sobering—in which rankism wreaks havoc in our lives. Consider the following examples in which national pride was damaged, lives lost, and billions of dollars wasted as a result of rankist mismanagement.

In the fall of 2004 at a talk I gave in New Jersey, a distinguished-look-
ing gentleman, who everyone present knew had served as the director
of both NASA's Goddard Space Flight Center and the Smithsonian
National Air and Space Museum, stood up and declared, "Rankism was
a major contributing cause of both shuttle disasters." In April 2005, Dr.
Noel Hinners elaborated for my tape recorder:

> The *Mars Climate Orbiter* mission failure in 1979 was due in part to
> what might be called technological rankism. It starts with an unques-
> tioning reverence for those who are anointed as experts or who assume
> that mantle on their own. All too often, they stifle discussion and quash
> dissension on technical issues—a form of technical intimidation.
>
> During the flight to Mars there were early warning signs that
> something was wrong in the trajectory analysis, but the navigation
> team wouldn't listen. When problems were pointed out they essen-
> tially said, "Trust us. We're the experts." Due to a software error, the
> spacecraft entered too low in the Martian atmosphere and conse-
> quently burnt up. This was foreseeable during the flight and could
> have been corrected, but we caved in to the insistence of the naviga-
> tion team that everything would be all right. That's technological
> rankism.
>
> A similar dynamic is well documented in the shuttle disasters. Prior
> to the *Challenger* flight, . . . engineers had warned that the unusually
> low temperature [in Florida the night before the launch] could be a
> problem for the O-rings. In this case, pressure by management to
> launch on time silenced engineering concerns. This wasn't techno-
> logical rankism; rather, it was garden-variety managerial rankism that
> led to one of our most vivid national disasters.
>
> The *Columbia* accident investigation report shows a similar phe-
> nomenon: "As what the board calls an 'informal chain of command'
> began to shape [the flight's] outcome, location in the structure
> empowered some to speak and silenced others."

These incidents, Dr. Hinners concluded, show that rankism can have
lethal consequences.

Examples of rankism at the corporate level have been making head-lines since the Enron collapse. Usually, they take the form of high-rank-ing executives enriching themselves at the expense of employees, shareholders, and lenders. But as the following instance makes clear, corporate rankism can kill.

After *Somebodies and Nobodies* appeared in print, people in the nuclear power business wrote to me about the rankist culture they saw in their industry, worried that if it wasn't changed, a disaster was inevitable. In the fall of 2005 the *New York Times* ran a story that sup-ported their fears.[2] It reported that employees at the Salem nuclear power station, near Salem, New Jersey, were reluctant to express con-cerns about safety because they were afraid of retaliation from their superiors.

Experts in the field warn that the rankist culture that pervades the nuclear industry poses a far graver risk to public safety than do the nuclear reactors themselves. Tish B. Morgan, with Booz Allen Hamilton, is an expert on nuclear power who has more than thirty years of expe-rience in nuclear licensing and regulatory issues, safety analysis, and advanced reactor design. In a recent conversation, she stated categori-cally that "rankism was the primary factor in what could have been America's worst nuclear disaster." She began her account with the acci-dent at Three Mile Island and then went on to describe an even more serious near-meltdown at the Davis-Besse nuclear plant near Toledo, Ohio, in 2002.

In 1979, just twelve days after the movie *The China Syndrome* came out, an accident at Three Mile Island seemed to be an example of life imitating art. During the several-day course of the crisis, rankism revealed itself in several forms—corporate rankism (which gave pri-ority to profits over safety procedures), technological rankism (hands-on operators bowing to outside nuclear "experts" who, it was later learned, were actually mistaken in their analysis), and regula-tory rankism, wherein "desk-jockeys" from the all-powerful Nuclear Regulatory Commission took control of the moment-to-moment operation of the plant and proceeded to make a bad situation far worse. Catastrophe was averted in the nick of time. But without rankism there would have been no incident and no stain on the reputation of the nuclear industry.

For more than twelve years, the management at the Davis-Besse plant dictated shortcuts and hurry-ups to keep it running (and thus making money). The result, discovered by accident during an oft-postponed inspection, was a rust hole caused by chronic leakage of boric acid into the reactor vessel head. Because management allowed only a preset number of hours for removing the acid, it had accumulated over time. The Nuclear Regulatory Commission later estimated that if the plant had continued to run without intervention, it would have suffered a meltdown within two to thirteen months.

Why, at Davis-Besse, did employees who had reported problems for years in the end just go along with what they believed to be unsafe operations? The answer is rankism, pure and simple, as in, "You do what I say, or else your replacement will."

The company, whose rankist practices almost gave us another Chernobyl, passed the costs of the near-meltdown—$800 million for a new vessel head and replacement power for the two years the plant was shut down for repairs—on to consumers. In addition, the parent corporation—FirstEnergy Nuclear Operating Company—has been identified as being primarily responsible for the wide-scale Midwest/Canadian blackout of August 14, 2003. Bowing to rankist orders, instead of disconnecting from the grid and trying to stabilize their own system, workers took other utility systems down with them. The economic impact of the blackout reached into the billions.

This chapter concludes with the mention of two very different, but no less deadly, forms of rankism: imperious fundamentalism and environmental depredation. When fundamentalist proselytizers, convinced that their doctrine bears the stamp of higher authority, adopt a superior stance toward nonbelievers, that's rankism. Fundamentalism's most familiar face is that of "true believers" who claim to know what's right for everybody. An extreme form of this is the kind of crusade or jihadism that those targeted call terrorism.

But fundamentalism has many faces. Others include scientific fundamentalism and its bullying insistence on the preeminence of purely technological considerations, and political fundamentalism, with its paternalistic certainty that it knows the needs of others better than they do. Other varieties of fundamentalism will be discussed in chapter 9.

Rankism's reach also extends to the environment—an arena in which rankist presumptions now threaten the very health of our planet. As creatures who exercise "dominion over the fish of the sea, and over the birds of the air, and over the cattle, and over all the earth,"[3] will we continue to sanction environmental degradation, or will we assume the role of responsible stewards? Will we exercise our "dominion" over animals in a manner that recognizes that they, too, are entitled to a measure of dignity, or will we tolerate their abuse and exploitation? Our responses to these questions hinge on our attitude toward rankism.[4]

A Way Out?

The issue at hand is not the seriousness of the problems humanity now faces—upon which most agree—but rather whether reframing them in a dignitarian perspective can give us new leverage in resolving them. The following chapters will show that building a dignitarian society by targeting rankism can indeed be an effective way to deal with the challenges confronting us. But first we need to take a closer look at human dignity and what form a movement to secure it might take.

DIGNITY AND RECOGNITION 2

ALL HUMAN BEINGS ARE BORN FREE AND EQUAL IN DIGNITY AND RIGHTS.
—UNITED NATIONS UNIVERSAL DECLARATION OF HUMAN RIGHTS

WE HOLD THESE TRUTHS TO BE SELF-EVIDENT, THAT ALL MEN ARE CREATED
EQUAL, THAT THEY ARE ENDOWED BY THEIR CREATOR WITH CERTAIN
INALIENABLE RIGHTS, THAT AMONG THESE ARE LIFE, LIBERTY, AND THE
PURSUIT OF HAPPINESS.
—THE DECLARATION OF INDEPENDENCE

TUCKED INTO THE opening lines of the U.S. Declaration of Independence is a phrase that, despite its ambiguity, has inspired people the world over for two centuries. Many have struggled with the meaning and implications of "created equal." Certainly, on the face of things, people are more easily seen as unequal, even at birth. In health, wealth, looks, talent, skill, and other qualities, it's obvious that we exhibit a wide range of differences. Moreover, as adults, our differences are often a continual source of the delight we take in each other.

By asserting that "all men are created equal," Thomas Jefferson, third president of the United States and principal author of the document, implicitly tasked the nation not only with protecting life and liberty but also with embodying fairness and justice. As historian Garry Wills argues in his book *Lincoln at Gettysburg,* when Lincoln invoked Jefferson's proposition in the first line of his famous Civil War address, he was implying that not just different individuals but also different races must be accorded equal rank.[1]

Jefferson, and Lincoln by quoting his words, were both asserting that people are equal not in their endowments or attainments but rather in their intrinsic value as human beings, in their dignity.[2]

Dignity: A Universal Human Right

Each of us has an innate sense that we have the same inherent worth as anyone else, regardless of our particular characteristics or our status. Every religion teaches us so. We experience this as a birthright, an immutable cosmic fact that cannot be undone by any person, circumstance, institution, or government. That is why rankism provokes such strong resentment—whether it occurs between individuals or groups, it is experienced on the deepest level as an affront to dignity.

Like any animal vulnerable to being preyed upon, we're supersensitive to threats to our well-being. Picking on the weak is the strategy of choice for all predators, and human beings have retained those instincts. Among our ancestors, those who missed signs of predatory intent became someone's lunch.[3]

For this same reason, we're alert to subtle attempts to determine our relative strength, from "innocent" opening lines such as "And you are . . . ?" or "Who are you with?" to more probing queries regarding our ancestry or education. All it takes is a faint whiff of presumed superiority or condescension and we're on guard.

Indeed, our dignity is often most easily discerned in the breach. We know at once when we're treated with disregard, and for good reason. An intimation or overt gesture of disrespect may be a feeler put out by someone to gauge the degree of our resistance to subordination, or to remind us of our place. For example, an insult is often a signal of intent to exclude the targeted individual from the group, to make him or her an outcast, a nobody. Likewise, an assertion of rank—even a subtle one—can signal an intention to dominate.

To be "nobodied" carries the threat of being deprived of social and material resources critical to our well-being. Such threats are tantamount to blackmail or extortion, forcing people to subordinate themselves so as to avoid the fateful consequences of ostracism. The need for dignity is more than a desire for courtesy. Dignity grounds us, nurtures us, protects us. It's the social counterpart of interpersonal love. To be treated with dignity confirms our status as a valued member of a group. Dignity and self-respect go hand in hand: dignity accorded us nourishes our self-respect, and a manifest self-respect inclines others to treat us with dignity.

In proclaiming a right to "life, liberty, and the pursuit of happiness," the Founders came tantalizingly close to making dignity a fundamental right. By liberty they meant freedom from arbitrary or despotic government or control. Therefore, the right to liberty, by militating against rankism, affords a large measure of protection to our dignity. Likewise, the right to pursue happiness is meaningless in the absence of the dignity inherent in full and equal citizenship. Hence, it's not that much of a stretch to find in the Founders' intentions an implicit, but as yet generally unacknowledged, right to dignity. The constitutions of Canada, Germany, and South Africa explicitly grant this right to all citizens.[4]

Who cannot identify with Shylock's rejoinder to affront in Shakespeare's *The Merchant of Venice*: "I am a Jew; hath not a Jew eyes? Hath not a Jew hands, organs, dimensions, senses, affections, passions?"[5] Or with the indignant protest of abolitionist Sojourner Truth: "Ain't I a woman?"[6] Both these pleas are demands for dignity. In each, the aggrieved speaker is laying claim to the status of full and equal membership in the human family.

Insults to dignity immediately shift our focus and divert our energy. The costs, whether expressed or suppressed, are high in every realm—the workplace, health care, education, and relations between individuals, groups, and nations. Most dangerously, chronic disrespect can set in motion a psychological dynamic whose end point may be violence and destruction. As Shylock continues, "If you prick us, do we not bleed? If you tickle us, do we not laugh? If you poison us, do we not die? And if you wrong us, shall we not revenge?" His warning concludes with the threat of escalation: "The villainy you teach me I will execute; and it shall go hard but I will better the instruction."[7]

A sports cliché has it that the best defense is a good offense. In life, an equally important component of a good defense is not giving offense in the first place. By protecting the dignity of others as if it were our own, we not only give them their due but simultaneously protect ourselves by preempting the desire for retaliation. Thomas Paine recognized this dynamic when he wrote, "He that would make his own liberty secure must guard even his enemy from oppression; for if he violates this duty he establishes a precedent that will reach to himself."[8]

Despite injunctions toward morality—like that implicit in Shakespeare's lines and Paine's admonition—and lip service paid to ethical behavior, history repeatedly demonstrates that morals are often ignored in practice, by the secular and religious alike. Had everyone honored the golden rule, segregation and other forms of racial discrimination would have been unthinkable and there would have been no need for the civil rights movement.

Though moral precepts may point the way, politics plays an indispensable role in actually changing human behavior. Political principles, as embodied in law, are essential if we want to close the gap that often exists between ethical ideals and common practice. A dignitarian politics gives teeth to the golden rule by making explicit a standard of compliance—equal dignity regardless of rank. It also calls to account those charged with enforcing this principle.

Given the remarkable achievements of the identity-based liberation movements, it's not unrealistic to imagine a day when everyone's equal dignity will be as self-evident as everyone's right to own property or to vote. (The current exception to the right to vote—people below the age of eighteen in most countries—will be addressed in chapter 5.) As others' right to dignity becomes axiomatic, our own responsibility not to insult their dignity becomes a corollary.

Indignity and Malrecognition

Peter Gloystein, economy minister in the state of Bremen . . . , poured wine over the head of homeless Udo Oelschlaeger during the launch of German Wine Week. "Here's something for you to drink," he said as he doused Mr. Oelschlaeger, who was standing next to the podium at the public, open-air event.

"Who are you? Why are you doing this?" a tearful Mr. Oelschlaeger retorted.

Mr. Gloystein, who was subsequently forced to resign his ministerial post, said he'd later met Mr. Oelschlaeger, who explained his difficult life. Mr. Gloystein apologized and they departed on friendly terms.[9]

The preventive for indignity and its many far-ranging consequences is recognition. What is required is an understanding and appreciation of each person's role and the contributions he or she makes to others and the world. These can be anything into which time, effort, and care have been put—a home, a scientific theory, a dance, a business plan, a garden, a cake, an office, or vacuuming the floor of that office at midnight.

Ultimately, it is through contributing to others that individuals, groups, and nations secure their dignity. For example, parental acknowledgment for setting the family table affirms a child's dignity. At the group level, the influence that African-American blues had on music is a source of black pride. The defeat of the German army on the eastern front during World War II remains a source of national pride to citizens of the former Soviet Union.

To be effective, recognition must be commensurate with contribution. Genuine recognition must be differentiated from false or inflated praise, which is experienced as condescension and can be worse than no recognition at all. The self-esteem movement fell into disrepute because the respect it offered was too often fake and exaggerated. Too much recognition for too little actually undermines dignity; we feel patronized. Likewise, disproportionately little recognition is experienced as disrespectful. Perhaps worst of all is denying people even the opportunity to contribute. That says to someone, "You are so obviously worthless that we're not even going to give you a chance to show us what you can do. You might as well not exist. Here, let me pour some wine on your head."

Recognition is to the identity what food is to the body—indispensable. By confirming our identity and affirming our dignity, recognition provides assurance that our membership in the group is secure. Absent this, our survival is at risk. Without recognition, individuals may sink into self-doubt and subgroups are marginalized and primed for exploitation.

Dignity and recognition are inseparable. We can't all be famous, but fortunately, recognition is not limited to the red carpet. We can learn to understand the effects on those who are either denied a chance to seek it or from whom it is otherwise withheld, and take steps to prevent *malrecognition*—that is, too little or no recognition at all—as we now do to prevent malnutrition.

Despite many attempts to eradicate the latter—and assurances from experts that it is actually within our power to do so—hunger and malnutrition persist.[10] Eliminating invisibility and malrecognition is no less daunting a challenge. But with respect to this task, we've only just begun. The science of malrecognition is in its infancy.

In contrast to malnutrition, malrecognition afflicts both rich and poor. Both maladies reduce the body's resistance to disease and lower life expectancy. For most people, just the opportunity to contribute something of themselves to the world is enough to stifle the inclination to lash out. This means that malrecognition, like its physical counterpart, is a preventable and treatable ailment.

One important place to treat malrecognition is in the criminal justice system. Work by Morgan Moss and Penny Patton, under the auspices of the Center for Therapeutic Justice, strongly suggests that treating prison inmates with dignity reduces the recidivism rate upon their release.[11]

A strategy of recognizing dignity can nip an escalation to violence in the bud. Below, a teacher describes an incident she witnessed in a post office, noting that the humble response, under stress, of the young man involved was indeed inspired:

> I was waiting in line. A young guy about twenty was at the counter buying stamps. Suddenly some ratty, crazed-looking man who was ahead of me in line started screaming obscenities at the guy. Young Guy turned around and said, "What? What did I do?" to the livid man, who screamed back, "You KNOW what you're doing!" like he was sensing evil rays coming out of Young Guy's forehead or something.

Young Guy kept saying "What?" and then he just stood there. Everyone in the room just froze up. It was extremely tense. Then Young Guy said to the crazed man, "I'm sorry, I didn't mean to disrespect you."

That comment was like a pin deflating the man's anger. He suddenly calmed down and backed off, because he felt he had his dignity back. An incendiary situation had been defused.[12]

Similarly, art therapist Candace Blase tells of standing in a crowd waiting for luggage at a carousel in the Sacramento airport. Nearby, two women were unself-consciously and loudly voicing their prejudices against lesbians. Candace turned to them and said, "I couldn't help but overhear your conversation. I'm a lesbian, and I don't think I'm that bad or dangerous." By speaking evenly, without anger or accusation, Candace made it possible for the women to take in and consider her words instead of defensively lashing back.

The supreme importance we attach to dignity and respect is revealed in, of all places, pirate life. Noah Brand, a writer who has studied the culture of buccaneers, explains:

Given that the life of a pirate was very tough, frequently involved no pay, and usually terminated at the end of a rope, why did so many seamen turn their backs on the navy in favor of piracy? The respectability and regular pay that came with a naval career was guaranteed, but these benefits came at the price of enduring chronic rankism. In the navy, discipline was rigid and rank was everything. You could get flogged for looking at the captain cross-eyed, and officers were often incompetent, sadistic, or both.

In contrast, on pirate vessels there were usually a few simple rules—concerning behavior, division of plunder, and so on—that everyone had to agree to in writing. From there on in, the majority generally ruled. Captains tended to be men of enormous personal charisma, because those who weren't were quickly replaced by more popular members of the crew.

That men would choose the short happy life of a pirate over a career of servile misery in the navy shows just how objectionable the experience of rankism can be. The chance to live, however briefly, as peers sharing an impossible dream trumps the security of living a long life as menials without hope.[13]

The hoards of ill-prepared young people dropping out of our schools today testify to the fact that we are still forcing many to choose between the short-term gratification of flouting the system and the long-term security that can be had by knuckling under to its routine humiliations.

As things stand now, when it comes to recognition, it's either feast or famine. A few individuals get the lion's share while a great many others must settle for crumbs. But unlike the supply of food, the supply of recognition is unlimited. Neither are there limits on the dignity we can accord to others. We needn't disparage Peter in order to acknowledge Paul. To increase the supply of recognition we need only discern people's contributions, acknowledge them appropriately, and compensate them equitably. Recognition is something like love: when we give it to others it comes back to us; when we withhold it from others, they respond in kind. The hallmark of a dignitarian society will be interpersonal, cultural, and institutional relations that provide recognition and dignity to all, regardless of circumstances or rank.

What Would a Dignity Movement Look Like?

In both business and government, many people act as if finding the right leadership is an adequate solution to rankism. That is like hoping the next king will be more benevolent than the last one. A more realistic assessment recognizes the need for broad popular opposition to rankism, just as the emergence of the civil rights and women's movements was required before substantive legislative inroads against racism and sexism could be made.

While the goals of the emerging dignity movement support and reinforce those of earlier social movements, the movement for dignity is unlikely to resemble the iconic televised images of movements past. That is because rank is defined *within* the various social and civic organizations. Therefore, attempts to overcome rankism are apt to arise within these separate institutions rather than "in the streets" in the form of an easily visible, unified social movement whose members share some trait.

The subordinate social rank once officially enforced on people of color in the United States is a prime example of rank illegitimately held. Rankism of this kind usually acquires a name of its own—racism, in this case—and is overcome by public demonstrations that defenders of the status quo perceive as a threat to the social order.

In contrast, when the dignity movement targets illegitimate uses of rank, it is likely to manifest not in million-man marches in the nation's capital, but rather in millions of schools, businesses, health care facilities, churches, and families across the country—that is, within the relationships and organizations in which rank is being abused. The specificity of rank—parent, coach, boss, teacher, doctor, rabbi, roshi, imam, or priest—means that a dignitarian society will be built relationship by relationship, organization by organization. The focus on rank—the locus of power—is exactly what gives this framework transformative power. The Greek mathematician Archimedes said, "Give me a lever long enough, and a fulcrum strong enough, and I will move the world."[14] Our lever is the will to dignity. Our fulcrum is a stance against rankism. Together, they can generate a force strong enough to change the world.

Contributing to the success of the trait-based liberation movements was support and leadership from individuals who were themselves not among the afflicted but who understood that it was in their own interest to help secure rights for those who were. Seminal roles in these movements, especially in their early stages, were played by fair-minded managers, unbigoted gentiles, white liberals, and nonchauvinist males, motivated perhaps by memories of having been nobodied themselves at some point in their lives. Regardless of their motivations, the dignity movement is also likely to depend heavily on help from a few enlightened leaders during its infancy. People of lower rank are reluctant to speak up unless it has been made safe for them to do so by someone with the authority to protect them if they take the risk.[15]

Stages of the Movement

The history of the women's movement for enfranchisement and liberation could well predict the stages of the dignitarian one. Movements
usually begin, as did the nineteenth-century and modern women's
movements, with the formation of small groups of people who share a
sense of injustice. In the 1960s, these consciousness-raising sessions
occurred in homes, schools, offices, and churches, primarily among
women. Within a few years, large numbers of women, along with their
male supporters, joined together in protest and mounted demonstrations on behalf of specific policy goals such as equal pay for equal work,
a woman's right to choose, the Equal Rights Amendment, and Title IX
(of the Education Amendments of 1972), which established school athletic programs for girls and women on a par with those for boys and
men.

Progress toward nonrankist, dignitarian values is likely to follow a
similar path. Much of the change will be set in motion in relatively private interpersonal conversations among victims and between victims
and victimizers within specific organizations. Through such discussions, those guilty of rankism will come to understand the impact of
their behavior on their targets, and some will be convinced to modify
it. Part of the incentive to change arises from empathy and an innate
sense of fairness, but by itself empathy is seldom enough. Also necessary
to produce real change is a vivid prospect of the negative consequences
of not doing so.

In the workplace, worker malcontent due to rankism inevitably
results in foot-dragging, which eventually shows up as reduced profits.
But the threat that the enterprise will lose out competitively is insuffi-
cient to change a culture of rankism if a leader is willing to sacrifice the
well-being of his organization to his privilege and stubborn pride. People of a certain age will remember Alabama's Governor George Wallace standing in the schoolhouse door defiantly shouting, "Segregation
yesterday; segregation today; segregation tomorrow!" to a national television audience. Likewise, the heads of some companies have preferred
to ruin their firms' reputations rather than give up the right to disre-

spect or exploit their employees. What it takes to get many leaders to alter their ways is the imminent prospect of forfeiting their jobs.

In another parallel with the identity-based liberation movements, the dismantling of rankism will be furthered by each of us examining our personal relationships with relatives, friends, co-workers, teachers, physicians, and religious leaders. The larger transgressions we complain about—corporate and governmental corruption; bullying in the workplace, the marketplace, and among nations—differ in scale but not kind from the "little" abuses of power most of us permit ourselves. As we prune our individual relationships of rankism we create the understanding, will, and confidence to challenge the broader forms of it that afflict society and the world at large.

As already noted, to create a movement you need to know both what you're for and what you're against. That is why the concept of rankism is essential. Without it a movement for dignity is toothless. Try to imagine a civil rights movement absent the concept of racism, or a women's movement without the concept of sexism. Until the targets of injustice have a name for what they're suffering, it is difficult to organize a resistance. In some situations, they may even blame their predicament on themselves and each other, never achieving the solidarity necessary to compel their tormentors to stop. Rankism begets rankism, so as surely as somebodies visit it upon nobodies, so too do nobodies inflict it on each other. A panhandler, spotting a copy of *Somebodies and Nobodies* I was carrying, insisted on telling me, "I'm not a nobody; I'm a somebody." Then, pointing to another street person about fifty yards away, she sneered, "See her? Now that's a nobody." Interpersonal rankism among the rank and file undermines their willingness to cooperate and unite against the more insidious forms of institutional rankism that marginalize them all.

As making the distinction between rank and rankism becomes second nature, and as rank is delineated and rankism disallowed, families will become more harmonious, schools will improve, and businesses will see greater productivity. When dignitarian institutions are the norm, those that remain rankist will handicap themselves in the same way that an avowedly racist institution disadvantages itself today.

A Dignitarian Business Model

Here's an example describing how a Seattle-area firm was transformed—in this case, from the top down—into a dignitarian institution.

In the early 1970s, residential real estate sales could charitably be called a predatory business. It was not quite as rapacious as in David Mamet's play *Glengarry Glen Ross,* but definitely not for the faint of heart. The tone was set by the principle of caveat emptor, which allowed sellers and their agents to misrepresent properties to buyers. That license characterized the conduct of the entire industry: agents abused not only buyers but sellers and each other as well; brokers in turn abused their agents. It was rankism at its rankest.

In 1972 John Jacobi bought a small local office in Seattle called Windermere Real Estate. A young man, he had resigned from a promising career in banking to escape the coils of bureaucracy. He had no brokerage experience but he brought a model of cooperation, not exploitation, and of dignity, not rankism.

Jacobi began dealing with his agents as equals and upgraded the appearance of their work spaces. He insisted that they conduct themselves with honesty and respect for all parties. He increased the agents' share of commissions and did nothing to encourage competition among them or, as the company grew, between offices.

These anti-rankist policies worked. Growth continued even in the grim years of the early 1980s, and today Windermere is a network of over 250 offices and some 7,500 agents throughout the West.

Jacobi's changes did not occur in a historical vacuum, however. Beginning in the mid-1970s, consumerism caught up with the real estate business and court decisions ended the practice of caveat emptor. The Federal Trade Commission forced profound changes in the industry, removing the stain of rankism from the relationship between agents and buyers.[16]

Although the analysis of rankism may at first seem more complex than that of the familiar isms, there is one way in which tackling it is actually easier: we all have known its sting. Not everyone has a personal experience of racism or sexism or the other isms, but because at one time or another each of us has been nobodied, there's a sense in which we've all set foot on the same boat.

But we are not yet all fully in that boat. Only as we opt to forgo the short-run gains of abusing a power advantage in exchange for a guarantee that our own dignity will be secure when the tables are turned do we align ourselves with others who've made this same choice. In time that solidarity group will assume the proportions of a movement which, as it swells, will force a renegotiation of the social contract predicated on the rejection of rankism. The result will be the creation of a legal framework for a dignitarian society analogous to that created by the U.S. Congress with passage of the civil rights and voting rights acts of 1964 and 1965, which paved the way for a multicultural society.

A second way in which targeting rankism simplifies matters is in the effect it has on the principle of political correctness. All of this doctrine's various, specific (and too often tedious) preachings can be replaced by one simple, comprehensive tenet: protect the dignity of others as you do your own.

Does this maxim sound familiar? The golden rule has been around for two millennia, but for the most part its observance has been optional and haphazard. Giving rankism a name and building a dignitarian society holds the promise of making adherence to the golden rule the norm rather than the exception. The reason this precept has always sounded unrealistically utopian is that there has not been a mechanism of accountability. Anyone could suspend it, at a moment's notice, to take advantage of a difference in power. This will be far more difficult, and hence far more rare, in a dignitarian society that expressly disallows rankism.

Even when people have the best of intentions, the feelings and interests of others are invariably hurt at times. We're constantly overreaching in our uses of power—stepping on others' toes if not their necks—and experiencing injury ourselves. But it's one thing to do this inadvertently and quite another to claim the prerogative to do it. Slavery and its segregationist aftermath were not defended as unintended deviations from the norm; they were defended in principle by whites who asserted their innate superiority and therefore their absolute right to dominate and exploit people of color.

So, too, rankism is now supported by many in principle. There will probably always be lapses, but once the burden of proof shifts from victims to perpetrators, we'll know that rankism has lost its sanction and a dignitarian consensus is in formation.

How can we hasten that day? First, by learning to anticipate which uses of power will cause indignity. We can do this by building a model of each proposed use of power in advance so as to predict its ripple effects. By interviewing those likely to be affected, we can avoid what would otherwise be attacks on their dignity. We keep revising the model until we find one that does no harm, and only then do we green-light the project. Today, environmental impact studies are routine. Why not "dignity impact studies?"

Second, we can take steps to eliminate rankism from our existing social and civic institutions. This means creating models of the organizations in which we live, work, learn, heal, worship, and govern ourselves, and then testing them in practice and adjusting them until they succeed in safeguarding the dignity of both those who staff and those who are served by them.

In building a dignitarian society, no tool will prove more valuable than modeling. Modeling has enabled humans to harness power and it can equally help us to limit its damages. The following chapter begins a discussion of models and their transformational role in human affairs.

WHEN FIRST WE MEAN TO BUILD,
WE FIRST SURVEY THE PLOT, THEN DRAW THE MODEL.
—WILLIAM SHAKESPEARE, *HENRY IV*

THE SCIENCES DO NOT TRY TO EXPLAIN, THEY HARDLY EVEN TRY TO
INTERPRET, THEY MAINLY MAKE MODELS. BY A MODEL IS MEANT A . . .
CONSTRUCT WHICH, WITH THE ADDITION OF CERTAIN VERBAL INTERPRETA-
TIONS, DESCRIBES OBSERVED PHENOMENA. THE JUSTIFICATION OF SUCH A
CONSTRUCT IS SOLELY AND PRECISELY THAT IT IS EXPECTED TO WORK.
—JOHN VON NEUMANN, DIGITAL COMPUTER LOGICIAN
AND CREATOR OF GAME THEORY

We Are Model Builders

THE TITLE OF Mark Twain's *What Is Man?* poses a question that human-kind has pondered for millennia. Over time, the species that scientists call Homo sapiens (the wise) has also variously been referred to as Homo faber (the builder, by Benjamin Franklin), Homo ludens (the game player, by Johan Huizinga), Homo economicus (the rationalist, by Adam Smith), and Homo babulus (the talker). Twain himself argued that man is a machine (Homo machinus).

While all of the above describe us, none does so uniquely. In fact, it seems that every time someone makes a case that a particular trait sets humans apart, experts in animal life say, "No, animals do that too."

Animals display intelligence, they build things (nests, dams) and use tools, they play games, make war, communicate, and have emotions.

Nonetheless, there is one faculty that humans appear to have developed more than other animals. It is our talent for consciously building models that represent nature, ourselves, and our institutions. Many of our models, both historically and today, take the form of narratives. Cooperating across the generations on the development of models and passing on our stories have combined to give our species a dominant role on this planet.

Model building, in combination with complex language, stands as one of humankind's epochal accomplishments. It's the faculty that has enabled us to harness nature's force. The flip side of this is that we often use these powers in ways that cause others indignity. But the modeling skills that have put power in our hands can also help guide us toward dignity-protecting applications of that power. The following paragraphs illustrate some of the key features of model building that will be used throughout this book.

Models Are Everywhere

People learn modeling early, starting with Play-Doh, Lego blocks, dolls, and model trains. The stories we grow up with are replete with models of human behavior. Teens today fancy themselves as video game characters and get to try out different behaviors vicariously, without risking their own lives or even punishment for "failure."

Scientists Francis Crick and James Watson modeled the double-stranded helical structure of the DNA molecule with Tinkertoys. There is a model of the San Francisco Bay—complete with miniature piers poking into the water, a scaled-down Golden Gate Bridge, and "tidal currents" propelled by pumps—that fills a warehouse in Sausalito, California. By studying it, scientists can anticipate the effects of proposed real-world alterations of the bay. Similarly, to protect Venice, Italy, from the rising sea, engineers use a model of the adjoining lagoon and gulf.

Using computers and mathematical models, weather bureaus the world over provide forecasts. As everyone knows, the predictions are not always right, but they're getting more accurate as the models upon which they are based improve.

Experimenting with model planes in wind tunnels enabled the Wright brothers to build the aircraft they flew at Kitty Hawk a century ago. Even more significant than the plane they built was their pioneering use of modeling in engineering. Models enabled them to anticipate problems through trial and error without paying the price of crashing a piloted plane. Today, flight can be simulated on computers by representing both the airplane and the atmosphere in a mathematical model.

Grand unifying models are the holy grail of every branch of science. In biology, Darwin's theory of evolution by natural selection is such a model. In chemistry, it's Mendeleyev's periodic table of the elements. In geology, plate tectonics accounts for all the earth's principal geological features.

Present-day physicists are searching for a "theory of everything" that would incorporate all known forces. "We hope to explain the entire universe in a single, simple formula that you can wear on your T-shirt," says Leon Lederman, a Nobel laureate in physics.[1] One candidate model, now under development, is string theory. Like all theories and models, string theory will ultimately live or die "solely and precisely," as stated in the von Neumann quotation at the beginning of this chapter, on whether its implications agree with observations.[2]

The use of models is not limited to science. Indeed, normative, prescriptive social models predate by many centuries the descriptive and predictive nature models just mentioned. Beginning in the distant past, cultural codes of conduct—for example, the Code of Hammurabi and the Ten Commandments—were used to govern family and tribal relationships. Other examples of social models include the charters, bylaws, and organizational charts of corporations, universities, and religious institutions.

Governance models of nation-states range from the divine right of kings to fascism, communism, and constitutional democracies. Entrepreneurs and the venture capitalists who invest in their companies are guided by business models that, by examining a range of scenarios based on various assumptions, forecast success or failure in the marketplace. Sometimes users of social models actually lose sight of the difference between their models and reality. As Alan Greenspan, longtime chairman of the Federal Reserve Board, warned: "A surprising problem is that a number of economists are not able to distinguish between the models we construct and the real world."[3]

When we use parents, heroes, public figures, and fictional characters as "role models," we're using models to shape our character. As will be discussed in chapter 11, religion gains its special place in human affairs by providing us with models of the self and its transformation.

In sum, models are descriptive or prescriptive representations of the world and ourselves, and they serve a variety of functions. Among these are to provide us a sense of identity, shape our behavior, maintain social order, and guide our use of power. Model building has made us what we are and holds the potential to guide us as we put our predatory history behind us and move into a dignitarian era. To see how models can help us make this transition, we need to familiarize ourselves with the broad features of the model-building process.

Models Evolve

Inherent in the notion of building models is that they change. That models are perpetually works in progress is a key reason why they are so useful. But it has been hard to accept the notion that models can and should change, yielding to modified or radically new ones as we gain more insight and information. Until relatively recently we have much preferred to stick to what we know—or think we know—and defer to existing authority and received wisdom. But ironically, our principal heroes are precisely those people who have struggled and suffered to overcome the notion that "the truth" is forever, usually by championing a new truth that contradicts the prevailing social consensus.

A turning point in the history of intellectual development came in the seventeenth century when one such figure, the English physician William Harvey, discovered that the blood circulates through the body. His plea—"I appeal to your own eyes as my witness and judge"—was revolutionary at a time when physicians looked not to their own experience but rather accepted on faith the Greek view that blood was made in the liver and consumed as fuel by the body. In persuading people to see for themselves, Harvey drove another nail into the coffin of Aristotelian fundamentalism, which had dominated thought for more than a thousand years.

As Bertrand Russell, the Welsh mathematician and philosopher, said, "Aristotle could have avoided the mistake of thinking that women have fewer teeth than men by the simple device of asking Mrs. Aristotle to open her mouth."[4] The idea that institutional dogma be subordinated to the empirical experience of the individual represented a critical juncture in human affairs. States quite rightly saw it as a threat to their monopoly on power. In fact, what we like to think of as the unassailable truth is actually just our best current understanding of things—in other words, our latest model. Nothing is more natural than that models should change with time.

Another classic example of the evolution of models was the shift from the geocentric—or Ptolemaic—to the heliocentric—or Copernican—model of the heavens. Until five centuries ago, it was an article of faith that the sun, the stars, and the planets revolved around the earth, which lay motionless at the center of the universe. When the Italian scientist Galileo embraced the Copernican model, which said that the earth and other planets revolve around the sun, he was abandoning the received wisdom of the church. This was considered sacrilege, and under threat of torture, he was forced to recant:

> I, Galileo Galilei, aged 70, arraigned before this tribunal of Inquisitors against heretical depravity, swear that I have always believed all that is taught by the Church. But whereas I wrote a book in which I adduce arguments of great cogency . . . that the sun is the center of the world and immovable, and that the earth is not the center and moves, I abjure, curse, and detest these errors and heresies and I swear that I will never again assert anything that might furnish occasion for suspicion regarding me.[5]

By maintaining that his arguments had "great cogency," Galileo defended his integrity while sparing himself the fate of some of his predecessors. The Dominican friar Giordano Bruno, an Italian philosopher-scientist like Galileo, was burnt at the stake in 1600 for championing the Copernican model. Fundamentalists have never lacked for conviction. As Galileo withdrew from the court, he is said to have mumbled, "But it does move." He spent the rest of his life under house arrest, making further astronomical discoveries and writing books for posterity. In 1992 an ecclesiastical commission appointed by Pope John Paul II finally and formally affirmed that Galileo had been right.

The Galileo affair was really an argument about whether models should be allowed to change without the church's consent. Upon the geocentric model rested a whole edifice of theological thought, much of which was also contradicted by new evidence. For example, finding seashells on mountaintops and fossil evidence of extinct species undermined theological doctrine that the world and all living things were a mere six thousand years old. Such discoveries posed a serious challenge to conventional wisdom and the authority of the church. Freeing ourselves from the idea that the world is fixed, immobile, and unchanging marked the birth of modernity.

Galileo's models were later improved upon by Newton, whose three laws of motion form the foundation of classical dynamics. Then, in the twentieth century, limitations were discovered in Newton's model. It works fine for falling apples and for space vehicles, but when applied either to objects moving at speeds comparable to the speed of light or to particles on the atomic scale, Newton's laws give erroneous predictions. These failings were overcome by relativity and quantum mechanics.

The twentieth-century theories do not invalidate earlier models. Rather, they stake out and provide road maps to new territory that prior models don't cover. Often, new models do not so much render old ones obsolete as circumscribe their domains of applicability, revealing and accounting for altogether new phenomena that lie beyond the purview of the old models. For example, relativity and quantum theory do not invalidate Newton's laws of motion. Newton's classical treatment still describes accurately the motions of the objects to which he originally applied them so long as they move at speeds much slower than the speed of light. NASA's space scientists have no need for the refinements of quantum or relativistic mechanics in calculating the flight paths of space vehicles. But if we wish to account for the dynamics of objects at very high velocities or describe atomic phenomena, we must use quantum mechanical models. For everyday-size objects moving at everyday speeds, the quantum and relativistic models reduce to the familiar models of classical physics. In sum, new models usually don't invalidate old ones so much as they transcend them.

This is also a key feature of the social and self models characteristic of dignitarian culture, which will be discussed in chapter 9. The idea of evolving truth is the lynchpin of such a culture. However, it's crucial to note that just because our models evolve does not mean that "anything goes." Indeed, quite the contrary: at any given time, what "goes" is precisely the best current model we've got. One simply has to be alert to the fact that today's best model may be superseded by an even better one tomorrow.[6]

Most contemporary students of the natural world are actually excited when they find a persistent discrepancy between their latest model and empirical data because they know such deviations signal the existence of hitherto unknown realms in which new phenomena may be discovered. The presumption that nature models are infallible has been replaced with the humbling expectation that they will eventually be replaced by more comprehensive and accurate ones.

If the past is any guide, we are unlikely ever to find a theory so comprehensive and accurate that it would bring an end to the search for more fundamental truths. Any model that seemed to account for all known phenomena would still be vulnerable to the possibility that new observations would reveal it to be incomplete.

Toward the end of the nineteenth century, many physicists believed they'd learned all there was to know about the workings of the universe. The consensus was that Newton's dynamics and Maxwell's electromagnetism together had everything covered. Prominent scientists announced the "end of physics." Then a few tiny discrepancies between theory and experiment were noted, and as physicists explored them they came upon all the previously unknown phenomena of atomic and relativistic physics. A new world was discovered and with it the technology that put its stamp on the twentieth century.

Albert Einstein believed that the final resting place of every theory is as a special case of a broader one. Indeed, he spent the last decades of his life searching for a unified theory that would have transcended his own landmark theories, reducing them to special cases of a grander theory. In postulating that the universe is "infinite in all directions," physicist Freeman Dyson suggests there will be no end to our explorations and that we are unlikely ever to come up with an all-inclusive model.[7]

This dynamic has its counterpart in social and self models. Instead of suppressing deviations from the current social consensus, we can examine them for clues that might lead us to a more encompassing synthesis, one that integrates previous experience with the new evidence. For example, when Alfred Kinsey's studies on sexuality revealed the full range of human sexual behavior, we faced two choices. We could label certain of these behaviors as perverted and try to suppress them. Or, we could relax our prescriptive models pertaining to sexuality and so accommodate them. The advent of reliable, available birth control only intensified the pressure for revising these models. The ensuing sexual revolution suggests that the public did in fact gradually move toward a different consensus on sexuality. That movement is still under way as the public comes to terms with homosexuality. Likewise, the worldwide controversy over same-sex unions has the potential to alter the traditional model of marriage.[8] In a growing number of countries, the debate has resulted in granting legal status to domestic partnerships.

Instead of repressing or ignoring a question or fact that challenges a current view of ourselves, we can welcome it as a harbinger of change. As we accept something about ourselves that differs from the norm, it is only natural to grant the same acceptance to others. For this reason, the idea of partial, ever-evolving truth is a keystone of dignitarian culture. Humility is not simply a trait to be admired; it's dictated by the incontrovertible fact that there are viable alternatives to our habitual ways of doing business. Given a chance to prove themselves, some of them may even turn out to be better than our own!

Models Are Commonplace

The notion of model building can sound technical at first, perhaps even esoteric. To make it clear that the use of this tool is not limited to scientists and philosophers but can be used expertly in "ordinary life," here is an example provided to me by writer and educator Dr. Pamela Gerloff, who reflected on her upbringing on an Illinois farm:

> I learned about model building from my mother. No one called it that; it was just what you did, the way you solved problems or made decisions, the way you lived in the world. If I asked my mother why I had to do something a certain way, she never said "because I said so," or even just "because." She always had a reason for why this way worked better than others. I was free to propose a different way—a different model—if I could come up with a more useful, effective, or efficient one, based on reason, observation, experience, or insight.
>
> Whether it was folding laundry, dealing practically with difficult (i.e., rankist) school officials, or understanding the complex psychology of human interaction, no model was static. Solutions and approaches changed and improved, and the superior model won out. I remember how her model for unloading hay bales from a wagon saved me from my own less effective approach, which had caused me considerable strain and struggle. ("I think of it as a puzzle," she said, as she gracefully selected the next bale most easily removed from the pile.)
>
> When I was a young adult interested in child rearing, she explained to me how, periodically, she used to secretly put new books on the bookshelf for her small children to "discover" on their own. She read philosophy and psychology, using others' thinking as a springboard to develop and refine her own theories about why the people we knew acted the way they did.
>
> It was exciting and adventurous, this way of approaching the world. No job was mundane, no chore particularly tedious. Everything was an opportunity for model building, for intellectual engagement. From my mother, I learned to observe, to contemplate, to formulate hypotheses and theories, to seek new and better solutions.

An example of the changing nature of social models is provided by the evolution of governmental models in the twentieth century. The United Nations Development Program reports that eighty-one countries moved from tyranny toward democracy in the 1980s and 1990s and that by 2002, 140 of the world's almost 200 independent nations had held multiparty elections—compared to just a handful a century earlier.[9] When we recall how few democratic states there were at the beginning of the twentieth century, a dignitarian world does not seem to be quite such an unrealistic goal for the twenty-first.

Ironically, the apparent infinitude of our ignorance about the universe and ourselves has an upside. In a perpetually unfolding reality, our business will always remain unfinished, our knowledge incomplete. We will never lose the opportunity to contribute by extending our understanding. Therein lies a transcendental refuge for human dignity.

Modeling Our Uses of Power

Only yesterday our forebears moved out of Africa. They multiplied and spread out across the earth. One tribe became many.

At every step of the way, we sought out nature's power and cleverly turned it to our purposes. We tamed fire, domesticated plants and animals, and built cities. By the time different tribes began bumping up against one another, they no longer recognized that we are all one family. They looked strange, sounded stranger, and inspired fear in each other. So under threat of enslavement or worse, we designed ever more potent weapons with which to protect ourselves. Sometimes, thinking we had the advantage, we turned them on branches of our estranged family. Over some five thousand generations we have accumulated enough might to return us all to the Stone Age. As Enrico Fermi, nuclear physicist and Nobel laureate put it, "What we all fervently hope, is that man will soon grow sufficiently adult to make good use of the powers that he acquires."[10]

Although Homo sapiens often misused their powers in the past, many of our species' misadventures can be chalked up to "youthful experimentation." How else to learn that certain actions have long-term negative consequences except by seeing what happens when we execute them? Moreover, on many occasions we have used power well. A species that can go from living in caves to landing on the moon in some tens of millennia must be doing some things right.

With luck, adolescence ends without serious mishap. But its inherent recklessness sometimes lands the young in trouble before they complete the dicey transition to adulthood. Because the powers we now command are capable of putting the entire human project in jeopardy, it has become ever more important that we learn to predict in advance the ramifications of their proposed uses. And we must institutionalize safeguards to minimize the damage should we miscalculate. When it comes to our use of power, building predictive models has become a matter of life and death. For example, based on models of global climate change, a scientific consensus is now forming that if we don't curtail greenhouse gas emissions, we may inadvertently induce a planetary catastrophe.

We took one step out of the Dark Ages as we ceased to accept the idea that authorities could make up the "facts" to suit themselves and began to substitute knowledge, evidence, and reason for hearsay, superstition, and dogma. Now we must bring the other foot forward out of the past. Today's challenge is distinguishing between rightful and wrongful uses of power. It's a distinction that goes to the heart of virtually all political issues, both local and global. The consequences of asserting rank range from the relatively harmless (as in the alienation of an acquaintance) to the fate of life on earth (as in global nuclear war or a man-made pandemic). We must begin to make a practice of refusing to acquiesce when people in positions of authority misuse that authority, even if we are the beneficiaries of their actions. Likewise, we ourselves must expect to be held accountable in this regard. By modeling the uses of power and choosing only those that protect dignity, we can do for standards of justice what modeling nature has done for standards of living.

Some might argue that we already accomplish this, albeit imperfectly, through the various mechanisms of democracy. It's true that democracy provides a recourse when government officials abuse their rank; we can vote them out. But thus far we've applied the democratic idea only to our civic affairs, only within national boundaries, and quite inconsistently. Democracy's next step is to extend its protections against rankism beyond civic affairs to social institutions and to relations among nation-states. As indicated in the preceding chapter, we can do this in two ways: (1) by conducting dignity impact studies before authorizing a new use of power, and (2) by remodeling existing institutions into dignitarian ones.

Rankism is invariably experienced, by the individual or group suffering it, as an insult to dignity. Indignity therefore provides us with a litmus test that signals a likely abuse of power. But determining which uses of power will damage dignity, and as a result, backfire, can no longer be left to the full-scale, rough-and-tumble tests of power politics. That has become too dangerous because modern weaponry is more destructive and more widely available than ever before. Rather, the process must be brought into the "laboratory," as natural scientists have learned to do, and modeled in thought or other small-scale experiments. As Stewart Brand puts it, "We are as gods, and might as well get good at it."[11]

Despite warnings from a few farseeing individuals, we have typically plunged ahead and learned only by doing. The end result has been the same as that suffered by the succession of foolhardy men who climbed into flying machines without first modeling the consequences of their designs: over and over again, we've crashed and burned. Conducting dignity impact studies in advance may sound far-fetched and utopian now, but this was once believed true of environmental impact studies, which are now mandatory. Nor are what we're calling dignity impact studies really a new thing. People do the equivalent every time they imagine the effect on someone of something they are about to do or say. Part of conducting ourselves thoughtfully—of not inadvertently giving offense—is projecting ahead before we commit ourselves to a course of action, especially when the stakes are high. Such imaginative thought-experiments have long been a common tool in model building of all sorts. It is now time to apply this tool systematically to our anticipated uses of power with an eye on their impact on dignity.[12]

By modeling the consequences of proposed uses of power, all of which hold the potential for unwelcome if not catastrophic results, we can disallow those that flunk the dignity test and thereby spare ourselves much grief. In doing so we'll be heeding Shylock's warning that victims of villainy are seldom satisfied with merely getting even, but rather are inclined to "better the instruction."

An Example from Higher Education: A Template for Remodeling Institutions

Although it's possible to delineate the broad features of a dignitarian society, no one can foretell exactly what shape they will take. Likewise, it's impossible to tell in advance precisely what an organization will look like after it is transformed into a dignitarian one. This is because the process of transformation must be one in which everyone involved has a voice and everyone's views have some political weight.

In a dignitarian society, the role of institutional architect is inherently collaborative. Providing a blueprint from outside the design process is contrary to the dignitarian spirit. This is not to suggest that the role of experts in education, health care, organizational development, government, and international relations is unimportant. Quite the contrary. But for the resulting institutions to embody equal dignity, these professionals will have to work directly with the people those institutions are being designed to serve.

That leaders and pundits insist on designing programs without involving those they're meant to serve is one reason their ideas usually fall flat. A paternalistic process is incompatible with a dignitarian outcome because such a process, no matter how benevolent, is inherently rankist. To illustrate the remodeling of an institution, the following is an example I'm familiar with—one from academia. Just change the names, and it illustrates the procedures that apply to transforming any kind of institution into a dignitarian one.

In response to the renascence of the women's movement in the 1960s, many academic institutions established special committees on the status of women. Typically, these committees were composed of women administrators, faculty, students, alumni, and staff, and also included a few men. They began their work by holding open hearings on campus during which anyone could call attention to policies or practices that were felt to demean women or put them at a disadvantage. The committees then compiled a list of specific instances of unfairness or abuse along with potential remedies and presented it to the administrator, group, or governing body with the power to redress the grievances at issue. Their final task was to persuade that official or body to adopt the recommended changes.

This process, widely employed to make institutions less sexist, can serve as a template for making institutions less rankist. Open hearings can allow participants to point out ways in which members of various constituencies feel their dignity is not respected. A portion of the complaints may be contested, with some eventually judged to be ill-founded and withdrawn or dismissed. A number of the valid ones will be relatively easy to address. Other problems may take years or even decades to rectify.

A few words of caution regarding committees—especially those charged with transforming an institution. First, the likelihood of success is greatly enhanced by the participation of a figure of very high rank in the organization who makes it clear that it's safe for others to seriously challenge the status quo. It need not be the president, but if not, it must be someone who everyone knows speaks for the president. Second, the committee must have a fixed deadline against which it works. As the postwar British Prime Minister Clement Attlee noted, "Democracy means government by discussion, but it is only effective if you can stop people talking."[13]

Dignitarian governance does not necessarily mean giving everyone a vote on every issue, but it does mean giving everyone a voice. To ensure those voices are heard usually requires having at least some voting representatives from each of the organization's various constituencies serving at every level of its governance. This is sometimes referred to as *multistakeholder* or *collaborative problem-solving*. For example, in an academic institution this means adding students and alumni to committees on student life, educational policy, appointments, and promotions, and to the governing faculty body itself and also the board of trustees. Typically, such representatives hold 5 to 15 percent of the seats, but the percentage could go higher. The aim is to ensure every group has an opportunity to make its interests known. This goal is given teeth by providing each group with enough votes to determine the outcome in those situations where the group as a whole is closely divided.

Vote ratios between various constituencies mirror their relative degree of responsibility for achieving each specific goal of the institution. Thus, students would have a decisive majority of votes on a student life committee, faculty a decisive majority on educational policy. And students, faculty, and administrators would all play minority roles in fiduciary decisions that traditionally are decided by the board of trustees.

Including voting representatives from all constituencies creates an environment in which the authorities do not merely deign to listen to those of lower rank. Rather, it behooves them to treat everyone with dignity because at the end of the day everyone will be exercising some degree of voting power over the outcome.

In addition to shared governance, a dignitarian institution is likely to possess a number of other distinctive characteristics. For example, the evaluation process would be broadened so that people from constituencies other than the one for which the person is being evaluated would be involved in hiring decisions and reviews of job performance. In the corporate world, such evaluation models are referred to as 360-degree reviews. All comments thus generated are provided as feedback to the employee. A growing practice is the appointment of an ombudsperson with broad responsibility for resolving disputes over the use and abuse of rank. Princeton University's ombudsman in 2004, Camilo Azcarate, told me that his job can largely be summed up as making the distinction between rank and rankism in a wide variety of circumstances.

Finally, institutionwide constitutional reviews would be scheduled—every five or ten years or more frequently if called for—to update the system of governance in light of changing circumstances to ensure that it remains dignitarian. As power evolves, new opportunities for abuse present themselves. No institution will remain dignitarian for long if it is not committed to coevolving with power.

The next chapter looks at how business organizations can be transformed into dignitarian ones.

DIGNITY IN THE WORKPLACE 4

THIS IS THE AGE OF THE RÉSUMÉ GODS . . . IN WHICH IT IS IMMORAL
TO DISCRIMINATE ACCORDING TO RACE OR SEX, BUT DISCRIMINATION
ACCORDING TO CAREER STATUS IS SO THOROUGHLY BAKED INTO SOCIETY
THAT IT GOVERNS EVERYTHING FROM RESTAURANT TABLE ASSIGNMENTS
TO ELEMENTARY SCHOOL ADMISSIONS PROSPECTS.
—DAVID BROOKS, POLITICAL COLUMNIST AND COMMENTATOR

A VITAL PART of leadership is the detection and elimination of rankism and malrecognition. Good leaders know this instinctively and seek to instill nonrankist behavior in others by exemplifying it in their own relationships with subordinates. As Jim Collins shows in his book *Good to Great: Why Some Companies Make the Leap . . . and Others Don't,* the founder-leaders of companies that excel neither indulge in abuses of power themselves nor tolerate it among the ranks.[1] They create an atmosphere of unimpeachable dignity from top to bottom in their organizations. As Robert Knisely put it: "For his book *Good to Great,* Jim Collins sifted through the 1,435 firms that have ever been in the Fortune 500. He found only 11 firms that demonstrated periods of exceptional performance. Notably, all 11 had CEOs who were . . . humble. 'Humble' is Collins's word, and by it he means a CEO who would listen to anyone, anytime, who might have something to offer to the CEO's quest for success. In other words, these CEOs eliminated every trace of rankism from their work lives—and they, and their companies, won big."[2]

Ten Ways to Combat Rankism in the Workplace

If companies that reduce rankism are more efficient and productive, the question becomes: How can rankism be rooted out of an organization? How can a corporate culture of rankism be transformed into a dignitarian one? Here are ten methods for doing so.

1. Recognize and Listen

Soon after his appointment as director of the Smithsonian National Air and Space Museum, Dr. Noel Hinners had an epiphany:

> I realized that the hierarchy was inverted—that the most important people, in terms of their daily contribution to the mission of the museum, were not those with the highest rank. To my surprise, it was quite the opposite.
>
> Ten million people visit the museum every year—the highest attendance of any museum in the world. When you have that many people tramping through your living room, it takes an incredible effort, for example, to simply keep the chewing gum off the floor. The janitorial staff did an unbelievable job keeping the museum clean and presentable. The security staff has to cope with the public and treat them with respect, but also make sure that no one vandalizes the exhibits. The education department was providing a service to a lot of school kids in the district. Without the restoration staff, which restores old airplanes and space artifacts to pristine condition, you couldn't put the exhibits together. And without the exhibits there was no reason to have the curators who do the research and collect the artifacts, and without them there'd be no need for my director's job.[3]

After having this realization at his first "all hands" meeting of the museum staff, Dr. Hinners acknowledged the importance of every job and the individuals who held them. Subsequently, he practiced "management by walking around," a tactic made famous by Mayor John

Lindsay, who walked the streets of New York City during the racial strife of the 1960s. Throughout his tenure, Dr. Hinners would wander through the museum visiting with employees. He says, "You don't know what goes on in an organization unless you meet people where they work, see for yourself, and listen, listen, listen." Obviously, making a display of listening is not enough. Leaders have to put what they hear to use and employees have to see that the information they are volunteering is making a tangible difference.[4]

Selectively ignoring subordinates sends a message of disrespect that can have unexpected consequences. At an open house for parents, the principal of a public elementary school in the San Francisco Bay Area introduced every teacher on the staff, save one. That woman, who taught computer use to over three hundred students, interpreted the omission as a snub deriving from her "instructor" status, which set her apart from the accredited teachers. The next day she submitted a letter of resignation in which she wrote:

> I feel this is a classic example of rankism. I am under contract as an instructor, but I am not being recognized in this position. In addition, I am not included on the staff e-mail list and yet I'm expected to attend meetings and make presentations without seeing the agenda ahead of time. If I am expected to act like a staff member, then why am I not treated like one? I enjoy my students and my teaching job very much. But I also feel that you must recognize my position as a staff member of this school.[5]

In this case the principal listened, perhaps because many of the staff, as well as parents, came to the defense of the aggrieved instructor. The principal not only apologized for her omission to the teacher—who subsequently withdrew her resignation—but also initiated an inquiry into rankism in her school. As is often the case, a single incident, and someone willing to put his or her job on the line over it, precipitated a broader transformation. But this happened only because the leader chose listening over defensiveness and turned an instance of malrecognition into a policy of respect.

2. Facilitate Questions, Protect Dissent

A fundamental characteristic of a healthy work culture is that everyone, regardless of rank, exhibits a questioning attitude. The freedom to challenge any action, any condition, and any assertion cannot be maintained in an environment laced with rankism. Only by continually demonstrating respect for all opinions and those who hold them will an environment be maintained in which a spirit of inquiry can thrive. Silicon Valley companies such as Intel and Hewlett-Packard, whose continuing success is vitally dependent on innovation, pioneered corporate cultures in which everything technical could be questioned by anyone, regardless of rank or seniority. The phenomenally successful Google has not only followed in their footsteps in this regard but breaks new ground in creating and implementing a nondiscriminatory workplace and a dignitarian corporate culture.[6]

The U.S. Navy nuclear power program employs the method of a *minority report*. Whenever a complex issue is under discussion and the answer is not obvious, a minority report must be prepared. Even if everyone agrees on an answer, the group leader asks someone to provide a report that presents the best case for the other side of the issue. Making it the manager's responsibility to seek a minority view lifts the burden and stigma from potential dissenters. Rather than discourage whistle-blowing, good managers create an open environment in which doing so never becomes necessary.

3. Hold People Accountable and Affix Responsibility

An indispensable element of a dignitarian work environment is accountability. In some highly technical arenas, errors in calculations can cost lives. Bridges have collapsed because of such mistakes. The important thing is to catch potential problems in a way that protects the dignity of workers so they won't be inhibited about voicing their concerns. In many engineering workplaces both the originator of the work and an assigned checker must sign off on calculations and drawings.

To qualify as a checker, a person must be capable of authoring the same work as the originator. At one nuclear plant, two signatures are required to issue a result. If it is later found to contain mistakes, the manager of the two individuals is informed. The manager in turn informs the two workers and records each name. Should one of the names emerge later as either the originator or checker on another calculation containing errors, a tick mark is placed by that person's name. You don't want to get that second tick mark. This is accountability in a dignitarian manner: the expectation of accurate work is conveyed at the outset and the consequences for anything less are applied equally regardless of rank.

Admiral Hyman G. Rickover, the creator of the nuclear navy, hung posters in his office and the officers' quarters that read:

Responsibility can only reside and inhere in a single individual.
You may share it with others, but your portion is not diminished.
You may delegate it, but you cannot divest yourself of it.
Even if you do not recognize it or admit its presence, you cannot
escape it.[7]

Creating a dignitarian culture in an organization—and ultimately achieving a dignitarian society—requires more than an absence of rankism. It necessitates understanding that responsibilities will vary with rank and station and that individuals must fully comprehend and own those responsibilities. A dignitarian society is one in which each of us is accountable to every other person for fulfilling the tasks we take on.

4. Incorporate "Flex-Rank"

Temporary rank-leveling is nowhere more prevalent than on the flight deck of an aircraft carrier. A strict hierarchy pervades every branch of the military. During an interview, Hal Gehman, chairman of the Space Shuttle Columbia Accident Investigation Board, remarked that people wear their rank on their sleeve, and authority is based on that rank, not on how smart you are or your length of service. A commander aviator is senior to a lieutenant commander aviator, even if the lieutenant commander is a better pilot. But once on the flight deck, a crew reorganizes itself horizontally. Everyone has a job and anyone is authorized to stop the whole process. When someone does this, that person is rewarded for stepping forward and is never chastised or second-guessed, regardless of his or her station. Flight crews are very hierarchical, but crew members can become peers at a moment's notice.[8]

This same flexibility is now practiced in the cabins of commercial aircraft. Formerly, the captain was treated like a god. Challenging his authority, even in dire circumstances, violated cockpit culture. However, after several fatal crashes that investigative bodies attributed to pilot error, a new system was developed. Known in the airline industry as CRM—Cockpit Resource Management—it encourages subordinates to raise any question at any time. The goal is not to undermine the captain's authority but rather to make it safe for other members of the flight crew to be more assertive, and when necessary, to override a captain who is operating the aircraft in a dangerous manner (for example, while intoxicated or when taking actions without the go-ahead from air traffic controllers).

As workplaces become dignitarian, rank becomes less rigid and fixed. While care must be taken not to assign it to someone lacking the necessary skill and competence, rank is likely to change on a task-by-task, or even hour-by-hour, basis. Faced with ever-shifting missions and circumstances, companies and organizations can reassign ranks to facilitate each new undertaking. There is no favoritism shown toward those temporarily serving in positions of high rank, and care is taken to protect the rights and privileges of those lower down on the totem pole.

5. Compensate Equitably

No organization can claim to be dignitarian if the ratio of the highest to lowest paid employees exceeds a certain number. What is that number and how is it determined?

The ratio is usually decided by the board of directors or by its committee on compensation. Typically, such groups include highly paid, high-ranking executives from other companies. If they are not already friends of the CEO or president, the latter are in a position to build and strengthen those friendships by lavishing attention and perks on board members. Sometimes outside compensation experts are brought in to advise board members on executive compensation, but the board members know it is management who butters their bread, not shareholders. The resulting inflation of executive salaries is implicit in John Kenneth Galbraith's wry and oft-quoted remark: "The salary of the chief executive of a large corporation is not a market award for achievement. It is frequently in the nature of a warm personal gesture by the individual to himself."

The average ratio of highest to lowest paid employees in the United States is in the hundreds. In Europe and Japan it is variously put at ten to fifteen, an order of magnitude less. It is rankism on the part of U.S. company directors, not the relative expertise of their CEOs, that accounts for this gross disparity. A dignitarian way to restore fairness in compensation is for the board to take into account the views of all stakeholders in the organization. In the corporate world, this includes employees, customers, and shareholders. In the academic world, it means students, faculty, staff, alumni, and perhaps a few representatives from the local community. In the nonprofit world, it is staff members, funders, and the community served by the organization.

Some companies have already begun the journey toward a fair compensation model that will be the centerpiece of a dignitarian workplace. *Newsweek* reports that at the grocery chain Whole Foods, executive salaries are capped at fourteen times the average worker's pay, leaving the CEO, whose stock holdings have made him a multimillionaire, with a salary of $342,000.[9] In the same spirit, Ben and Jerry, the ice cream gurus and founders (and principal shareholders) of their successful firm, have limited their own salaries to seven times that of the janitors. Though these steps toward a dignitarian workplace are unlikely to be enforced when founders no longer control a company, they nonetheless represent significant milestones.

And what such trailblazers find when they give their workers a voice in management decisions and a stake in earnings is that the enterprise and everyone involved in it reaps significant benefits.

6. Delegate

Dennis Bakke, the author of *Joy at Work,* describes the company he cofounded and led—AES Corporation, a leading independent producer of electricity—as "a workplace where every person, from custodian to CEO, has the power to use his or her God-given talents free of needless corporate bureaucracy. . . . Every decision made at the top is lamented as a lost chance to delegate responsibility—and all employees are encouraged to take the game-winning shot, even when it isn't a slam dunk."[10] Bakke describes a model of a company that treats employees with respect, delegates power, and holds those who assume it accountable, and argues that this all makes good business sense.

7. Break the Taboo on Rank

Among the twenty "Breakthrough Ideas for 2005," the *Harvard Business Review* lists "A Taboo on Taboos."[11] These include such old, familiar risqué subjects as sex, death, and God. But one taboo remains—one still too hot to touch in corporate America—and that is rank. Rank is the elephant in the boardroom and on the factory floor. As with other elephants that have sat in our living rooms, bedrooms, and schoolrooms over the years, we can learn to talk about it and in so doing relieve a lot of pain and eliminate dysfunctionality. We've learned to discuss race, gender, and sex. So, too, can we learn to discuss rank—its rights, its responsibilities, and especially the limits to those rights and responsibilities. Unless we talk about rank, we are powerless against rankism.

Once rankism is on the table, it's harder to get away with it. The moment politicians recognize and acknowledge it as a problem, any rankism on their part will be seen as hypocrisy. And if there's one thing voters dislike in their public servants, it's hypocrisy.

Breaking the taboo on openly addressing the subject of rank and learning to recognize and call rankism by name are prerequisites to exposing our uses of power to public scrutiny and subsequently rejecting any that are judged likely to inflict indignity. This is what it means to build a dignitarian society.

8. Be Transparent

Opacity, censorship, and secrecy are rankism's handmaidens. What can't be seen, what goes on behind closed doors, what's recorded in closed books, can't be effectively evaluated or criticized.

A simple thing like open budgeting can allay suspicion, yield savings, and create a sense of communal trust. We opened the books at Oberlin College when I was president during the 1970s and after a flurry of interest during which people satisfied themselves on various counts, attention shifted to other matters. But knowing that anyone could examine the budget at any time kept administrators on their toes and eliminated chronic distrust on the part of students and faculty. If a doubt arose at some point about finances, those concerned could just go see for themselves. This put a damper on rumor-mongering, too, because we could always point to the actual figures.

The secrecy in which compensation packages are typically cloaked in most organizations gives those who are privy to this information—high-level managers—an unfair advantage over everyone else. Extending transparency to budgets and compensation discourages favoritism, one of the most invidious forms of rankism.

9. Flatten Unnecessary Hierarchies

Although rank often serves a valid purpose—clarifying levels of authority and expediting decision making—when it's not needed to get the job done, its existence alone can foster rankist practices. All too often rank functions primarily to provide a specious rationalization for unwarranted distinctions in status, salary, and perks. Gerard Fairtlough's book *The Three Ways of Getting Things Done: Hierarchy, Heterarchy, and Responsi-*

ble Autonomy in Organizations describes various models, from pyramidal to flat, and the conditions under which each works best.[12]

One way to get rid of rankism is, of course, the one that has long been promoted by egalitarians—eliminating rank altogether. My favorite example of an organization that went this route is the Juice Bar Collective in Berkeley, California, where I often get lunch. At this small business, which provides takeout dishes made from scratch, each of the nine members is paid the same $14 per hour and each has one vote on policy. Old-timers get a little deference from newer members when it comes to hours, but not much and not for long.

When I ask what it's like to work there, everyone says pretty much the same thing: "It's a family. We each have our own opinions but we're very supportive of each other. We're working for ourselves and none of us ever wants to work for a boss again." The newest member of the collective told me, "What a great business this is! I am a one-ninth owner of the enterprise. I love everyone I work with. It's hard work but it's also wrong to call it work. It's worth making less money to be happy and on equal footing in your work life." One old-timer volunteered: "We think about the customer's health. We care about the people we're feeding. The customer is always right, but if one of them is outrageously rude we reserve the right to tell them to go home and cook their own food. We do not feel we deserve to be abused by customers who feel they aren't being served fast enough. We are human beings and we are giving you food and you are not higher than we are. That's the feeling of working at the Juice Bar."

Not far from the Juice Bar sits the Cheese Board, a sister collective founded by the same people and run according to similar principles. It sells cheeses from all over the world as well as bread and bakery goods made on the premises. Recently, as I paid for a scone, I asked the cashier what it's like to work there. She replied, "It's nice. I've been here for fifteen years. We own the place." Then she looked up with a wry smile and added pointedly, "We're *not* disgruntled workers!"

These two examples offer valuable models of successful small businesses with flattened hierarchies run by happy employees who are proud of their products. Dignity is implicit. It even seems to rub off on customers—a notably contented lot.

What about issues of diversity in a dignitarian workplace? The diversity that is increasingly common in today's work environment makes ridding the workplace of rankism all the more important. Abuse and discrimination that might be taken for granted between people in the same identity group are likely to be magnified when they involve people of different race, gender, and so on. As Art Kleiner, editor-in-chief of *Strategy + Business*, writes:

> A growing body of academic work substantiates the presence of rankism and its destructive impact. Research by Toni Gregory of the Fielding Institute strongly shows that the ability to create a diverse workplace depends on building up the mental and emotional health of the people who work there, from the executives on down. Dr. Gregory says, "Rankism is one of the key blocks to . . . diversity-maturity: that emotional growth which a diverse workplace requires."[13]

Dr. David A. Thomas, an expert on diversity at the Harvard Business School, points out that businesses, in their haste to treat a diverse workforce equitably, lose something when they create a corporate culture that inadvertently promotes sameness and suppresses cultural differences.[14] As rankism is identified and rejected and dignity becomes secure, the differences that diversity brings to the workplace are welcomed. The next step beyond a diverse workplace is a dignitarian one wherein cultural differences can be celebrated and tapped for the wisdom inherent in them instead of blandness being promoted out of fear of reigniting old prejudices.

A final example of flattening unnecessary hierarchy is provided by the decentralization practiced by MoveOn, the Internet-based, nonprofit political action group. The "MoveOn Way" is described by cofounder Wes Boyd:

> MoveOn staff live all around the country, and no two people work in the same location. This is not an accident. It's an experiment in radical decentralization, sometimes called the "virtual office," that we believe has been an important part of our success. The experiment began when we engaged our first core team members and didn't

require any of them to relocate to San Francisco. We soon discovered that decentralization gave us important advantages over traditional organizations.

Facilities are a major part of just about every organization's cost structure. Because we have no headquarters, we can put the money saved into benefits for staff. Since we live wherever we want in the country and work at home, this saves hours of commuting time. In addition, MoveOn reimburses people for home office space and expenditures, which helps them afford a good place to live. Benefits like these are a great recruitment tool. They enable us to hire the best applicants for the job, no matter where they reside.

It's very important that we are not centered in Washington, D.C., and that we are truly populist. MoveOn staff are "embedded" in the communities that make up America. Our work is not our entire life. As social beings, we pursue the healthy development of community and connections outside work. This delivers the extra benefit of helping us avoid the trap of hyper-activism in which our only experience of the world is with people who think like us.

We believe that decentralization works—but we are not inflexible. There are times when employees do need to be in the same place at the same time. We make exceptions for (1) periodic retreats for developing strategic plans and reconnecting as a team, (2) training periods for new staff, and (3) crash projects. But these times must be short and defined, and do not lead to the establishment of hub offices. No power centers are permitted—a practice which fosters fair and equal treatment for everyone.

One of the pitfalls of political activism is assuming an elitist posture toward the rank-and-file membership. MoveOn's commitment to a flat and decentralized organization supports us in approaching our members the same way we must approach each other—respectfully.[15]

In addition to flattening unnecessary hierarchies, there have been some dramatic examples of flattening illegitimate hierarchies by what can perhaps be described as an "over-my-dead-body" strategy. This occurs when a somebody comes to the defense of a nobody who is being abused by another somebody, and in effect, says to the bully, "If you attack him, you attack me. I stand with those you are victimizing and together we shall stand you down."

In his book *Exodus,* Leon Uris tells the story of King Christian X of Denmark, who adopted this strategy to undermine the imposition of an illegitimate, rankist social hierarchy under the Nazi occupation. As the author tells it, when the German occupiers ordered Jews to sew yellow Stars of David to their sleeves to mark them for discrimination, expatriation, and as we now know, extermination, the Danish king had the star sewn on his sleeve and encouraged all Danes to do likewise.

The veracity of this story has since been questioned, as the Jews in Denmark were evidently never forced to wear the Star of David. But another tale, which is accepted as truth, tells of King Christian's successful resistance to the swastika being flown over the Danish parliament. The king summoned a senior Nazi official and told him to take down the flag. When the official refused, Christian is reported to have said, "A Danish soldier will remove it." When the German replied that the soldier would be shot, the king's reply was, "I think not. For I shall be that soldier." The German flag was removed.

I mention these stories not simply because they are moving but to demonstrate two things: First, we love people of high rank who use the power of their rank to serve a group for which they have responsibility, especially when doing so places them in jeopardy; and second, there are times when the only person who can challenge a rankist offense is someone who outranks the perpetrator.

10. Consider Peer-to-Peer Organization

Networks are replacing hierarchies everywhere you look. Michel Bauwens sees peer-to-peer (P2P) networks as the premise of a new mode of civilization. He describes them as "a form of organization which rests upon the free cooperation of equipotent partners performing a common task for the common good, without recourse to monetary compensation as the key motivating factor, and not organized according to hierarchical methods of command and control."[16]

Examples of this kind of collaborative peer production include the Internet, digital file sharing, grid computing, blogs, open source operating systems such as Linux, the open access encyclopedia Wikipedia .org, and Web-based organizations such as Meetup.com, Newstrust.net, Worldchanging.com, and Sourceforge.net.[17] Intelligence is located everywhere within these entities.

P2P networks have antecedents in human history. Juries are a form of peer governance of long standing. In classical Athens, as well as medieval Florence, issues of war and peace were decided by public assemblies.[18] An emerging noxious kind of P2P organization consists of networks of small, autonomous terrorist cells. Their nonhierarchical structure makes them less vulnerable to attrition and decapitation, and presents a resilient, robust target for the militaries charged with neutralizing them.

In business, two new developments—the abundance of information and new digital technologies—are making P2P networks competitive with, if not superior to, the centralized hierarchical models that now predominate. Bauwens sees P2P networks as the technological framework of *cognitive capitalism*—the successor to merchant and industrial capitalism. He argues that they signal the emergence of a new form of power in which expertise can unexpectedly announce itself as needed, and in which participants are rewarded for giving knowledge away because doing so builds their reputation. Individuals who join a P2P project subordinate personal gain to building a common resource that is legally protected from usurpation by any one contributor. Eventually, common ideas emerge that represent a synthesis of the contributions of the many.

The characteristics and architectures of P2P networks, as well as their limitations, are not yet fully understood. But it is already clear that in some contexts, the budding open source movement is giving traditional hierarchies a run for the money.

Open source communities see themselves as pure meritocracies. But while the abolition of rank automatically eliminates certain blatant kinds of rankism, it can mask jockeying for status. Most common is an atmosphere of aristocratic noblesse oblige. "Newbies" may be snubbed by old-timers of proven repute and have to undergo a long apprenticeship before their ideas are taken seriously. As in more traditional organizational models, people who feel insecure are more likely to mount challenges to the dignity of others in order to find out where they themselves stand.

Other problems that typically plague nonhierarchical models are stagnation and lapses in responsibility. It is silly to argue that hierarchy or heterarchy or P2P is always the better model. The real question is: What kind of organization is best suited to getting the job at hand done and done well? Once that decision is made, it's important to bear in mind that rankism can rear its dysfunctional head in one way or another in almost any kind of institution. It won't be eliminated simply by redrawing the organizational chart.

When the Boss Is a Bully

The film *9 to 5* depicted a nasty boss. More recently, *Mean Girls* showed how "popular" girls are sometimes bullies in schools. In 2005, a presidential nominee for U.S. ambassador to the United Nations had his appointment stalled because of subordinates' allegations of his bullying. Bullying is archetypal rankism, and it's ubiquitous. What's new is that it has suddenly become newsworthy. This suggests we may be approaching a tipping point in regard to its public acceptance.

Here are some facts about bullying in the workplace, as excerpted and paraphrased from the Acorn Center's Web site (www.workthatworks.ca):[19]

- ▶ A recent study estimates that approximately one in six U.S. workers directly experienced destructive bullying in the preceding year.
- ▶ Supervisors may use bullying to swat down a threatening subordinate, or a manager may look for a scapegoat to carry the department's or the boss's frustrations.
- ▶ Some bullies target subordinates for the sheer pleasure of exercising power . . . a kind of low-grade sadism. They often start on one person and then move on to someone else.

▶ Malicious bosses often elicit from their subordinates defensive habits first developed as children, such as reflexive submission and explosive rage. "Once these behaviors lock in, people are transported to a different reality and can no longer see what's happening to them and cannot adapt," according to Dr. Mark Levey.

▶ Ambition of co-workers is the most insidious ally of the bully. Frequently, when workers witness a boss humiliating a colleague, they are relieved that they themselves are not the target and wonder if the victim did not in fact deserve the treatment. In that case, according to Dr. Calvin Morrill, "The brutal behavior goes unchallenged, and the target feels a sudden chill of isolation. By doing nothing, even people who abhor the bullying become complicit in the behavior and find themselves supplying reasons to justify it."

▶ Based on U.S. figures from 2003, 58 percent of bullies in the workplace are female, 42 percent are male. Woman-on-woman bullying represents 50 percent of all workplace bullying; man-on-woman, 30 percent; man-on-man, 12 percent; woman-on-man, 8 percent. Since bullying is same-sex harassment most of the time, it is often invisible when seen through the lens of antidiscrimination laws.

The vignettes that follow—personal stories posted on the breakingranks.net Web site—illustrate the damage done by workplace bullying. From Oregon, Roxanne, a woman in her mid-fifties, laments:

I have worked as a legal assistant for over three decades. My current bosses (one man, one woman, both my age) have no compunction about screaming obscenities to my face, ordering me about and refusing even the most urgent requests for time off (such as when my dad died or when I sustained an eye injury). Because they are high-profile and well connected, the chance of my obtaining other employment in this relatively small legal community is about nil. I lack the money to leave the area so I stay and endure the situation.

What's frightening is the prevalence of this type of abuse. An article in a national law magazine notes that "legal assistants are coming out of these firms like whipped dogs." An apt simile, and evidently not about to change—or have you ever tried suing a lawyer?

The next story, from an anonymous post to breakingranks.net, illustrates the high cost of standing up to rankism.

> While working as a low-level associate in a prestigious architectural firm, I experienced severe rankism. I have never been more humiliated and denigrated. My boss was an authoritarian who made life there a living hell for me and many others. The "higher-ups" were well aware of her malicious harassment, yet indirectly encouraged it through inaction. I came to understand the stories I'd heard about the many others who'd held my job before me and why it was a "revolving-door position."
>
> One day I asked a co-worker who was leaving the wood shop to pick up after himself because the mess he left was becoming a hazard for others. He took offense at this on grounds of his seniority, complained to *his* superiors and as a result, I was summarily fired.
>
> I've been job hunting for almost a year now. I was discarded like an old magazine and lost my health insurance. Because of my low rank in the firm I was considered inconsequential and easily replaced. No consideration was given to how this would affect me as a fellow human being trying to get along just like anyone else. We live in a culture of rankism.

How to combat such rankism? The answer is both personal and institutional. This story from Sylvia Cope of Port Orange, Florida, shows how even a modicum of economic independence empowers people to defend themselves against rankism on the job.

> I prepare transcripts for court reporters on a freelance basis. The expected hierarchy is lawyer, court reporter, scopist (me). But since we are all self-employed, I never bought into any notions of relative worth and importance. I feel that my labor is equal in value to anyone else's, that the mere fact that someone is better compensated

does not make that person superior to me. I have sometimes felt an undercurrent of resentment directed toward me because of my independent attitude. I know they want me to be a handmaiden, but I am fortunate enough to be able to choose to work only for people who respect me. I am acutely conscious, however, of how tough it is for those who have no other option but to put up with disrespect and antagonism.

By maintaining your dignity in the face of rankism you can sometimes stare it down. A forty-one-year-old office worker in Seattle writes:

After reading *Somebodies and Nobodies,* I quit a job full of rank abuse to find one that was free of it. In interviews I specifically asked about this issue and was pleasantly surprised by the interest in it. Not long after I accepted a position as development director for an interfaith association, it became clear to me that a long-term staff member was an unconscious rankist. In the absence of a name for her habitual disparagement of co-workers she'd been allowed to "just be her" for way too long. Her subordinates were miserable. But after we began to discuss the subjects of somebodies and nobodies and of rankism and dignity, her behavior changed markedly for the better.

Two years later, the same woman wrote again:

It's not just that my relationships with my superiors, my co-workers, and my friends have been changed—my relationship with myself has changed as well. Once my experiences with rankism were illuminated, I could understand why I had always felt frightened and unsure. Now I'm more confident and willing to stand up for myself. I've even enrolled in college—something that was unthinkable before.

It is essential to understand that rankism cannot be ended with more rankism. It can only be ended when people find a way to protect the dignity of their tormentors while at the same time suggesting to them a way to treat others with respect. The following success story is from a thirty-five-year-old salesman at a Silicon Valley company who had taken a management job—director of strategic alliances, at almost double his old salary—at a large, well-established software company. His response to chronic bullying there helped a perpetrator break an ingrained pattern of abuse toward his subordinates.

My enthusiasm quickly faded when I realized my boss, Ross, was a tyrant. My inability to confront him early on and establish my independence enabled him to become increasingly unpleasant. He would:

▶ Cut me off midsentence during meetings with my colleagues.
▶ Discount my opinions.
▶ "Forget" to include me in conference calls with my partners.
▶ Force me to provide him with a detailed, to the minute daily plan.
▶ Question my intelligence and dedication.

Ross gave his team impossible goals and went ballistic when they weren't achieved. For over a year I thought about quitting despite the fact that the dot-com implosion had decimated the job market. But the very day I planned to announce my resignation, Ross began redirecting his wrath toward someone else.

Then, after six months of relatively good treatment from him, there was a blowout. He came by my desk yelling some unreasonable demand, and when I protested, he became extremely aggressive and started verbally attacking me. The next time I saw him, I insisted that we go to Human Resources together. I was nervous and angry and once there, I realized my actions could cost me my job.

At first Ross was composed and pretended to be nice. But after about an hour his rage began to appear and it became obvious to the director of HR and even to Ross himself that he had unintentionally put his aggressive nature on display. He managed to calm himself and the meeting then took a turn: both he and I began treating one another with more respect. He even praised me for how much I'd grown and what a good job I was doing, while I acknowledged that his management style had improved prior to this last blowup.

This ended my difficulties with Ross. From then on he treated me with kindness and respect, and subsequently, when his stature in the company declined, I even felt sorry for him. I've never witnessed a more profound transformation in someone's personality. My experience with Ross taught me that rankist people can change.

A monthly newsletter with items on workplace and school bullying, posttraumatic stress disorder, psychiatric injury, and information about conferences and books on these subjects can be found online at bully-online.org. Further evidence of the negative effects of bullying appears in a study published in the *Journal of Applied Psychology* in December 2002. It shows that rank-and-file members of the Air National Guard with abusive supervisors were more likely to perform only the minimum required of them. And in a study published by the *Journal of Occupational and Environmental Medicine,* also in December 2002, researchers found that the number of sick days taken by hospital employees bore a marked correlation to their perception of fairness—or the lack of it—in the workplace. There can be little doubt that abusive bosses are bad for both the health of workers and the bottom line of companies that employ them.

Academia and Civil Service

The instititution of tenure was established in response to arbitrary firings by administrators, often for personal or political reasons. Protecting workers and teachers from administrative rankism was and remains an essential goal. By broadening the group of secure individuals, tenure diffuses dominance hierarchies, and that's to the good. But achieving these ends by granting lifetime job security creates another problem—one whose financial cost has become unsustainable and whose moral cost, especially to the far greater numbers of the untenured, is no longer defensible. It is time to find a better solution to the vital need to enhance and extend academic freedom.

To be legitimate, rank has to be earned in a fair contest with all qualified comers. In practice, this means periodic requalification because with the passage of time, there are new aspirants who may be more competent. In violation of this principle, academic tenure gives professors a job for life just as civil service tenure does for government workers, regardless of their ongoing performance.

Nonaccountability is a recipe for rankism. Recipients of tenure may well have earned and deserved renewal of their contracts, but lifetime appointments effectively bar others from even competing for those positions. The consequences for young applicants to a tenure-track position are no different from those that racial and gender discrimination has on blacks and women. Tenure now functions as the equivalent of a perpetual "Sorry, No Vacancy" sign to countless legitimate contenders for academic positions. John M. McCardell Jr., president emeritus of Middlebury College, Vermont, observes: "Why must institutions make a judgment that has lifetime consequences after a mere six or seven years? . . . Why not a system of contracts of varying length, including lifetime for the most valuable colleagues, that acknowledges the realities of academic life in the twenty-first century? . . . Today, almost every negative tenure decision is appealed. . . . Few if any of these appeals have as their basis a denial of academic freedom."[20]

Of course, academic and political freedom must be guaranteed. But as McCardell points out, there are now more effective ways to do this than by bestowing lifetime job security. Until an alternative is implemented, colleges and universities will resort to the appointment of so-called adjunct faculty to avoid making long-term commitments. Adjunct professorships carry a fraction of the pay, no benefits, no role in governance, no job security, often not even parking privileges. Many of the people in these positions are as well trained and as capable of conducting research as tenured faculty. Their ranks are further augmented by poorly paid graduate student teaching assistants. To have two categories of teachers working side by side—one privileged and secure, the other exploited and expendable—with the underpaid group subsidizing the prerogatives of the other is reminiscent of segregation in America and apartheid in South Africa. Those who are marginalized—adjuncts and teaching assistants—are hamstrung in fighting this injustice by their own reluctance to take on the real culprit, the tenure system itself. The forlorn hope of joining in the spoils of rankism—in this case, the privileges of tenure—often functions to keep downtrodden individuals from teaming up to oppose the institutionalized rankism that keeps them down as a group.

Another hidden cost of tenure is to students and taxpayers. Since pay goes up with seniority, the institution of tenure results in an increasingly expensive faculty or civil service. The result in academia is to price higher education out of reach of the middle class, let alone the poor, and in society as a whole, to make our bureaucracies far more costly to taxpayers than they need to be. Without tenure, there would be more young faculty with junior-level salaries and fewer older professors with senior-level ones. The resulting savings could be used to increase the affordability of higher education. Some senior teachers are important as repositories of experience, wisdom, and institutional memory, but lifetime tenure for, typically, two-thirds of the faculty results in top-heavy, overly expensive institutions.

Likewise, without tenure there would be fewer civil servants with decades of seniority and correspondingly high salaries. When certain jobs, and the individuals who hold them, are exempt from market forces, the people those workers serve invariably end up having to pay too much.

The burden of keeping a university solvent and affordable to students should not fall disproportionately on its adjunct faculty and teaching assistants. Their cheap labor is an involuntary gift to tenured faculty and long-term administrators in the same way that the nonacademic working poor subsidize entire societies. Forced benefaction is indentured servitude by another name.

Ridding academia and the civil service of rankism presents all teachers and all civil servants with the same challenges: earn your job; re-earn it periodically in fair, open competition with other aspirants; remain accountable to your peers and customers.

What deserves and needs protection is not peoples' jobs, but their dignity. Since a loss or change of job can leave one vulnerable and subject to disrespect, attention needs to be given to protecting the dignity of people making such transitions. As this kind of support is institutionalized, pathways will be established from the academic to the business world and vice versa, and from one specialization to another. In-house faculty placement offices will spring up alongside those that help students find jobs. And retraining programs will be created in the recipient institutions.

Universities can undertake to design alternatives to tenure and institute placement programs that would protect the dignity of their present faculty and staff before the growing crisis hits them full force. That it will do so shortly is not in doubt. To glimpse the future, one has only to look at the soaring costs of the traditional college degree and the growing enrollments in Internet-based education.

Nations that manage to remove rankism from their civil service and their educational and business institutions and establish dignitarian workplace environments will gain a competitive advantage over those that do not. Dignitarian environments are good for the bottom line because as rankism is reduced, the commitment and energy that individuals bring to their jobs increases. Eradicating rank-based discrimination and injustice pays dividends in the form of greater loyalty, higher productivity, and fewer days of sick leave.[21] Negative motivations such as fear of ridicule, demotion, or dismissal are dwarfed by the positive incentive that comes from being recognized as an integral part of a skilled, flexible, and responsible team. As the hidden costs of rankist management become clearer, an antiauthoritarian model will spread through all our social institutions.

An Example from the World of Dance

One might think that dancers, as stars, are immune to workplace abuse. But in an e-mail dated October 1, 2005, Claire Sheridan, founder of Liberal Education for Arts Professionals (LEAP), an innovative program to address the problem, noted that this has not been the case.[22]

The workplace culture of ballet has a sorry history. Traditionally, dancers are expected to tolerate abuse and insults from artistic directors and choreographers, work in pain, and live in poverty. They rou-

tinely sacrifice their education. Adult professionals are still called
"boys" and "girls." And when injuries end their career (usually by age
30), most dancers, ill-prepared for the future, are simply dismissed
with no pension.

One way to address this kind of rankism in the ballet world is to
make it possible for dancers to get a college education. Having one
changes the way professional dancers see themselves. While developing the skills needed to succeed in life after dance, they learn that they
can be successful in other areas, and as a result, they are not as willing
to put up with workplace abuse because they know they have options.

However, dancers usually join the professional ranks before they
are 18, and many are employed by companies that require them to
work six days a week as well as go on tour. In this extremely competitive field, these artists can't take four years off to attend college during their prime dancing years.

In 1999, I founded a bachelor of arts degree program called LEAP
(offered by Saint Mary's College of California) to address this problem. LEAP removes the barriers that prevent professional dancers
from getting a college education. For example, the class schedule
accommodates the work, touring, and rehearsal calendars of the
dancers. Classes are held at hotels near theatre districts and dance
studios. The program offers individualized courses of study and an
affordable tuition, and a strong support system provides encouragement and guidance.

There are now more than a hundred dancers enrolled in LEAP, and
the program is spreading nationally. Education has enabled dancers
to see themselves as somebodies and demand dignity in their workplace. Fears that participating dancers would be "distracted" (i.e., not
focused on their careers) proved to be unfounded. Recognizing that
a more confident, educated dancer is a better artist, ballet administrators are now very supportive of LEAP. Some have even enrolled in
the program themselves!

This example provides a good transition to the following chapter,
which focuses on learning.

DIGNITY IN EDUCATION 5

I'M AFRAID OF DYING BEFORE I PROVE THAT I'M SOMEBODY.
—TYONDRA NEWTON, A TEENAGER RAISED IN FOSTER HOMES

ONE OF THE clearest indications that we are—at least in some areas—already moving toward the dignitarian ideal is the remarkable evolution of child-rearing practices that has occurred since the 1960s. Well into the twentieth century, "Because I say so" was considered reason enough for forcing a child to submit to almost anything. But over the last several generations we have moved from children being "seen but not heard" toward an increasing parity between the young and their elders—not in knowledge or experience, of course, but in their status as persons.

Kids Are People, Too

"Kids are people, too" is the slogan guiding this transformation. The generation that came of age in the 1960s—known to the world as the baby boomers—will someday be recognized not merely for its size and appetites, but for adopting a new model for bringing up children. It will be known as the first generation to grant youngsters equal dignity with adults, and in so doing initiate what is arguably one of the most significant emancipations in human history.

Of course, all liberation movements produce a backlash. The Russians lamented the unruliness of serfs who were granted their freedom, and former slaveholders in the American South denounced "uppity

Negroes." A landmark book titled *Backlash* portrays attempts to roll back gains made by the women's movement,[1] and more recently, voters in one American state after another have rejected gay marriage. In light of this, it's no surprise that many complain that the revolution in child rearing has produced a generation of brats.

But listening to the young and taking their views into consideration is not the same as indulging them or abdicating parental responsibility for their well-being. It seems quite possible that we are witnessing a historical shift that, within decades, will make it unthinkable to abuse or dominate people just because they are not yet full-grown. The result will be a generation of young adults that assumes dignity as a birthright and passes it on to *their* children.

One example of the new attitude toward youth is that public authorities have begun to intervene in family life if they perceive a child to be in danger. Abuses that used to be shielded from public scrutiny with a defiant "Mind your own business" are now being exposed and eliminated. In the service of protecting children, parental sovereignty has been circumscribed.

It's plausible that the next step toward affording children equal recognition as individuals will be to find a way to factor their interests into electoral politics. Democracy's mantra of one person, one vote is well overdue for an adaptation that gives weight to issues that matter to the young. Many of the arguments for denying them a voice in political matters—which obviously affect them profoundly—sound very much like the old paternalistic rationalizations for denying women and ethnic minorities equal rights. Respecting children's dignity in politics is an important part of teaching them to respect the dignity of others when they reach adulthood.

Obviously, when it comes to those below a certain age, the notion of them personally casting a vote is absurd. A different mechanism will have to be designed. But once the idea is embraced philosophically, building an electoral model that comprehensively implements "one person, one vote" will not be an insuperable task.

As life spans increase and the population grays, failure to make the franchise more age-inclusive will result in national ossification. Likely effects of granting the young a role in electoral politics will be an increase in support for education and for natal care. In Germany, where there are now more people over fifty than under twenty, it is argued that giving weight to the interests of the young is necessary to encourage parenthood and arrest the slide into gerontocracy. Otherwise, an aging population is likely to vote itself a greater share of society's limited resources at the expense of the disenfranchised young. This will harm a country's capacity to innovate and create. It's a recipe for national decline.

Learning with Dignity

There's a reason why educational reforms, whether progressive or conservative, invariably leave many of the young withholding their hearts and minds from study. What's sapping their will to learn is the unacknowledged rankism that pervades educational institutions from kindergarten through graduate school and beyond. In a rankist learning environment, the need to protect our dignity drains attention away from acquiring knowledge and skills. For many, chronic malrecognition has undermined self-confidence by the age of six and taken an irreversible toll by the age of twelve. As William James wrote in *The Principles of Psychology:* "With no attempt there can be no failure; with no failure, no humiliation."

Students in rankist schools are like ethnic minorities in racist schools: they will sacrifice learning if they feel they must do so in defense of their pride. For blacks this can mean resisting what they see as the "white way." For students in general it often means refusing to do things the "right way," as held up to them by teachers and parents.

Tragically, avoiding humiliation trumps personal growth. The life-long consequences of rejecting the system often seem preferable to another day of submitting to disgrace in the classroom. By minimizing the potential for denigration, we can spare children from this fateful dilemma. As we become more attuned to signs of malrecognition and take steps to address them, we can expect significant improvements in the capacity of students to learn.

The actor Henry Winkler, an advocate for people with learning disabilities, claims that two-thirds of the inmates in our jails and prisons have this problem. It's plausible that the chronic indignity to which their disabilities exposed them as youths is a factor in their high rate of incarceration. Why? Because as already discussed, the cumulative effect of indignity is indignation, and if the kettle blows, the result can be jail time.[2]

An example of gratuitous humiliation and the lingering pain it can cause is provided by the thirty-five-year-old managing editor of an American publishing firm.

My father was a marine biologist with the United Nations. One of his first postings was to Qatar. The only English middle school in the country was private, and the sight of dark-skinned South Asians like my father and me was new to the Europeans and Arabs there.

Applicants for admission were interviewed by the school principal, Ms. Beanland. She was the epitome of the colonial headmistress, possessed of that crisp English elocution that lets you know immediately that she sees you as beneath her. She asked me to read aloud. As the son of a highly educated South Asian, I spoke English as well as the other seven-year-olds did, but as a native Tamil speaker educated in Sinhalese schools, I lacked the British accent Ms. Beanland required.

Three sentences into the reading she held up her hand: "Stop! I cannot understand you!" She then called in a girl and asked her to read the same paragraph. Annabelle had a beautiful British accent that brought a smile to Ms. Beanland's face. She clapped as her prize pupil finished and then, in Annabelle's presence, informed my father that admitting me would pose a risk to the education of the other children.

My shame and anger were compounded by the almost grotesque combination of humiliation, rage, and resentment I saw on my father's face. But since Ms. Beanland was the principal of the only English school in the country, he dared not object. I have never felt as low and inconsequential as I did that day.

The indignity suffered by my father filled me with resolve to fight back. For six months I worked with a tutor to bring my accent "up to par." Then we returned and when the same test was administered, I passed. I made a point that year of getting higher grades than

Annabelle. My father and I never spoke of the incident, but I know it gnawed at his soul, as it does at mine.[3]

Imagine how this story would have turned out if the boy had not had an educated parent possessed of resources with which to oppose the principal's rankism. Most students are undefended against such denigration. It's small wonder that many become discouraged and lose confidence in themselves.

Aptitude tests can be a tool for helping guide the young toward a vocation suited to their interests and abilities. But that tool is misused if, instead of serving a constructive, diagnostic purpose, tests are employed to stigmatize those who do poorly and exalt those who do well. Guidance counselors must be careful not to use educational ranking as in the past—to effect and maintain a division between "winners" and "losers" and reconcile the latter to their station via humiliation and invalidation.[4] When that happens, test scores become self-fulfilling prophecies and eventually an unbridgeable gap is created between students destined for success and those marked for failure. If the young are not actively discouraged, and instead allowed to pursue their interests as far as they're internally impelled to, they will often be able to realize their goals in one form or another. The world has a way of giving more accurate and useable feedback than professionals guided by scores on one-time tests given under what are often artificial and adverse conditions.

Physical education classes have long been a scene of embarrassment and humiliation, especially for those who are not natural athletes. The executive director of the National Association for Sport and Physical Education, Charlene Burgeson, maintains that memories of gym class discourage many adults from incorporating exercise into their lives. Although she believes that "for the most part we have eliminated the humiliation factors" from physical education classes, she warns that "we cannot practice in a way that leads to embarrassment for students. It's counterproductive."[5]

What's true in gym class is equally true in reading, writing, and arithmetic. There's a good reason why Billie won't learn: Protecting one's dignity comes before learning. However, if we create a dignitarian environment in which it's safe to do so, students will not hesitate to put their bodies and their minds fully to the test.

As already emphasized, although rank is not inherently rankist, it often becomes so in practice. Whatever the goal of the enterprise—to teach, to build, to heal, to protect—the burden of proof should be on those with rank to show that it's necessary to accomplish the mission at hand. To safeguard against rank's tendency to overreach and rank-holders to self-aggrandize, we must seek out and adopt the least hier-archical model compatible with delivering the best product or service.

Antibullying Projects

Bullying is increasingly recognized as pervasive and destructive. In recent years, it's begun to be addressed where many first encounter it: in the schools. Some 160,000 students in California miss school every day out of fear of attack or intimidation by other students. Twenty-seven percent of California students are harassed because they are not "masculine enough" or "feminine enough."[6] Following are descrip-tions of four projects designed to put bullying in the spotlight and then eliminate it.

Somebodies and Nobodies in a Public School

In the fall of 2004 Stephanie Heuer, an instructor in a public school in San Jose, California, came up with a novel approach to the problem of bullying. She wrote two short phrases on the chalkboard:

I feel like a nobody when. . . .

I feel like a somebody when. . . .

She asked her pupils, grades 2 to 5, to complete these phrases—only if they chose to and without giving their names—and then made a book of their responses. She got 100 percent participation. Here's a sampling of what the children wrote:

I feel like a nobody when:

▶ Somebody calls me stupid.

- ▶ My mom and dad are yelling at me.
- ▶ People don't play with me.
- ▶ My father doesn't listen to me.
- ▶ My parents fight.
- ▶ I am not invited to a party.
- ▶ My mom doesn't say goodnight. It makes me feel invisible.

I feel like a somebody when:
- ▶ People play with me.
- ▶ People listen to me.
- ▶ I help someone.
- ▶ I do something hard.
- ▶ I am loved by my mom.
- ▶ I get all my homework right.
- ▶ I do well on my vaulting. (I want to give someone a big hug.)
- ▶ Everyone in my family does something together.
- ▶ I feed my dog and cats.

A few other responses:
- ▶ I felt like a somebody when I got a new pair of ballet shoes that were white. I felt pretty the first time I danced. I felt like a pretty somebody.
- ▶ I feel like nobody most of the time. My dad isn't here anymore. I feel like somebody when he comes back to visit. We get to play ball.
- ▶ I feel like nobody when I am me; I feel like somebody when I am you.

Timeless and universal, these statements speak for children everywhere, and for many adults as well. As people realize they are hurt in the same ways and made happy by the same things, they begin to treat others differently. Transforming institutional procedures into dignitarian ones is what's ultimately required to safeguard dignity, but knowing how others feel and recognizing ourselves in them comes first.

Following are some other pupil responses and Stephanie Heuer's report on how these comments changed the way she conducts her classes:

"I feel like a somebody when my parents congratulate me." **Change:** If students apply themselves—for example, if they have achieved a "personal best"—Heuer now acknowledges the effort even if it's not among the best in the class.

"I feel like a somebody when the teacher calls on me when I raise my hand in class." **Change:** Kids just about burst when they know the answer and are not called on. She now has everyone who knows the answer shout it out at once. The ones who don't are not singled out, and those who do experience the thrill of participating. Many kids have come up and told her how much more fun this is.

"I feel like a nobody when I get left out of a game." **Change:** She has made the recess staff aware of this and all try harder to see when it is happening. Once they began looking they discovered that a core group of about ten kids were being consistently ignored at recess.

"I feel like a nobody when math problems are too hard." **Change:** Now when she gives a complex assignment, Heuer first shows it to the group as a whole and then devotes some one-on-one time to students for whom it is difficult. Also, students can anonymously write a question on an index card and drop it into a jar, and she'll review it the next day in class.

"I feel like a nobody when others whisper and laugh about something I did." **Change:** If she sees or hears of this, she takes the whispering kids aside and has a chat with them. Before she understood how hurtful this was, she just ignored it.

"I feel like a nobody when I have to read out loud in front of class." **Change:** Heuer notes that "this was a big one for me" because it was written by one of her own daughters. Now she tries to be very aware of who she calls on in class and if she anticipates any problems, she'll let students know the paragraph ahead of time to allow for practice. Then she asks them to tell her when they're ready to be called on. This has been 100 percent effective. Kids prepare without other children knowing their little secret and everyone does better.

"I feel like a nobody when other kids make fun of my clothes." **Change:** The PTA got parents to donate clothes that their children had outgrown but were still in good condition. If administrators see a child with worn-out or inappropriate clothes, they offer them a chance to pick out "new" ones.

"I feel like a nobody because my nana went to heaven last year. I miss her. She always read me stories." **Change:** Teachers are alerted by staff when a death occurs in a family. Heuer talks with her students privately about their dad or grandma and what they liked about them, and so on. They are free to write something about the person who died instead of their usual assignment.

From her students' responses, Heuer created an illustrated book for use in schools. For more information, visit her Web site at www.somebodybook.com.

The No Name-Calling Week Coalition

The No Name-Calling Week Coalition promotes one simple idea: *Words hurt.* Words have the power to make students feel unsafe to the point that they are no longer able to perform well in classes or conduct normal lives.

The coalition aims to create safer schools by making bullying, denigration, and name-calling unacceptable. It does this through public education campaigns that motivate youth to change their behavior and mobilize students and educators to take action around the problem of verbal harassment. The Web site is www.nonamecallingweek.org/cgi-bin/iowa/all/about/index.html.

Girls and Bullying

Thanks to books like *Queen Bees and Wannabes* (on which the film *Mean Girls* was based) and *Odd Girl Out*, we now recognize that bullying is an equal opportunity activity—girls do it, too—and that it comes in subtler forms than the extortion of lunch money under penalty of a bloody nose.[7] Suze Rutherford travels all over North America giving workshops to school administrators and teachers entitled "Unmasking Rankism: Changing the Tolerance of Disrespect in Our Schools" and "Odd Girl Out: The Ways Girls Bully." She does this under the auspices of YES (Youth Empowering Systems) of Sebastopol, California.[8]

Operation Respect

Operation Respect is a nonprofit organization dedicated to creating safe, caring, and respectful environments for children. Founded by folksinger Peter Yarrow of the group Peter, Paul, and Mary, it distributes educational resources designed to reduce the emotional and physical cruelty some children inflict on others through ridicule, bullying, and violence.

When kids are asked in class if they have ever been humiliated in public, typically all hands go up. The students are surprised to learn they are not alone, that the problem is universal. Operation Respect has developed a curriculum for schools to train teachers how to convince children of the hurtfulness of certain behaviors. It is already being used in twelve thousand American schools and camps.[9] Peter Yarrow's song "Don't Laugh at Me" serves as Operation Respect's anthem.[10]

One-Upmanship and Elitism in Academia

When I was in college, a book called *One-Upmanship* was circulating that defined the practice of keeping one step ahead of others by appearing to have better information, connections, possessions, or experience. As it turned out, that little book provided a more accurate model of higher education than did the college catalog. *One-Upman-*

ship was to academics what Machiavelli's *The Prince* was to politicians—a survival guide.[11]

Although knowledge was worshipped, the business of passing it along was often profaned. For many students and professors the primary satisfaction lay not in the learning and teaching but rather in ranking the abilities and contributions of others and honing their skills at targeting the dignity of presumed inferiors. As one stung by the disdain of fellow students, I never suspected that even the brightest were ill-served by this snobbish atmosphere.

Recently, I came across some remarks by Alexandre Grothendieck, a German-born French mathematician who came of age in the midtwentieth century—and whose impact on mathematics is compared to that of Einstein's on physics. Listen to his lament:

> Mathematics became a way to gain power, and the elite mathematicians of the day became smug, feared figures who used that power to discourage and disdain when it served their interests.
>
> The competitive, snobbish attitudes of the upper crust of the mathematical world contrasts with the service to the mathematical community of writing clear and complete expositions that make fundamental ideas widely accessible. The mathematical community lost this sense of service as personal aggrandizement and the development of an exclusionary elite became the order of the day.[12]

Grothendieck argues that such an atmosphere stifles creativity and renewal. He believes that innocent, childlike inquisitiveness gives birth to the creative impulse and he mourns the way it is trampled on by the desire for power and prestige. He traces his own creative capacity to "the naïve, avid curiosity of the child . . . who has no fear of being once again wrong, of looking like an idiot, of not being serious, of not doing things like everyone else."

Creative elites often cultivate an air of superiority and mystery, and resist sharing their knowledge and wisdom. I remember my shock when I read in the preface to a well-known mathematics text the author's promise to give away the trade secrets in his field, and my growing amazement and gratitude as I discovered he was actually keeping his word.[13] Much science and mathematics teaching is needlessly obscure, with obfuscation serving the purpose of limiting membership in the "guild." Similarly, some spiritual teachers have been known to substitute mystification for clarification, thereby ensuring that their students do not become a threat to their authority.

Elitism comes in a variety of flavors. A brief description of polar opposites—Princeton, where I did my graduate work in physics, and Columbia, where I had my first teaching job—illustrates this.

Princeton had an Old World feel. Einstein had died just months before I got there and his spirit hung over the place. The professors behaved like gentlemen, and research into big, timeless questions set the tone. Academic robes were required at dinner in the graduate college. In contrast, Columbia was imbued with the manic, competitive energy of New York City. The professors vied openly with each other and research focused on more concrete issues of immediate consequence to physics and careers.

At departmental lunches, Columbia professors would make "futures" bets on one another's chances for a Nobel Prize: "$10,000 now for half your Nobel winnings if you get it"—that kind of thing. One battle-scarred professor summed up his feelings about a lifetime of racing-for-the-roses research with a quote from Genghis Kahn: "It is not enough for you to succeed; your colleagues must fail." I admired him for daring to put into words what was in fact a common attitude.

At Princeton, the competitiveness was no less intense, despite being more discreet. In the oak-paneled tearoom, colleagues spoke reverently of the mysteries of the universe, but an undercurrent of one-upmanship lurked behind the pleasantries. If you asked a question, you had to be prepared for a condescending put-down like, "Oh, that's trivial," followed by a breezy snow job that left you more confused than ever. Knowledge is indeed power, and some, afraid of losing their edge, are loath to share it.

Despite their different styles, the scientific goal at both Princeton and Columbia was the same: to build models that accounted for the physical evidence, that predicted something new, and that suggested experiments that could be performed to confirm or disprove the theory. Fortunately, among the faculty in both departments there were some whose aim was to help you become the best scientist you could possibly be. Apprenticing with them was an exacting but exhilarating experience. I can't imagine a better way to absorb the mysteries of any field than working alongside a generous master.

Two recent stories, personal e-mail communications sent to me in October 2005, illustrate what can be done when professors indulge themselves at the expense of their students. The first, from a second-year journalism student, demonstrates the common strategy of going over the head of the offending party. The second shows that in many cases, rankism need only be pointed out in order for it to be cured. From the journalism student:

In my school, one professor stands out as the most feared writing teacher. He hates excuses. "Better never than late" is his favorite saying.

In a class last semester, he started off as tough and harsh as ever. But gradually he began criticizing students personally—rather than just critiquing their work—and rambling on about the stupidity of other professors. The class was dismayed, but because he was shielded by his prestige and position and because he had control of his students' grades, no one dared to confront him.

Finally, a group of three classmates decided to speak to the department chair, who immediately arranged a meeting between the professor and a few of his peers. The faculty members first acknowledged the offending teacher's years of accomplishment and service, but then made it clear that a growing number of people found his behavior abusive. The following week, the professor apologized to his classes and his behavior improved markedly, as did his mood. Because the chair and faculty approached their colleague with respect, he responded in a positive way. They managed to get relief for the students, correct the errant professor, and strengthen the entire department.

Now the second e-mail:

One of my professors had an extremely bad habit. During classroom discussions, when a student was trying to present an idea or ask a question, he'd often cut them off midsentence and give us *his* view of things. At first, we didn't really perceive this as a problem. His knowledge of the subject was vast and his speaking style almost addictive. Listening to him was such a pleasure you'd almost forget that he wasn't listening to you. But eventually we realized that we weren't getting as much as we ought to from the sessions.

Finally, three of us went to the professor's office and explained the situation to him. I'm convinced that our approach was responsible for our success. We began by emphasizing our immense respect for him and made clear that we didn't think he was interrupting us on purpose, but that it was affecting us adversely. The look of embarrassment that passed over his face was awful to behold. He genuinely did not realize what he'd been doing. Classroom discussions immediately improved.

As an invisible ailment, rankism is easy to miss. But once identified it can sometimes be cured by nothing more than the offending party's basic sense of decency.

Society pays a terrible price for sponsoring institutions that force students to sacrifice their dignity in order to learn. Tragically, our schools merely reflect societal practices that force the same choice on everyone. The indignities of schooling in the early years keep many from acquiring even the basics and most from realizing their full potential. Once established, the right to dignity will be as empowering in education as the right to vote is in governance.

Educating a Population of Model Builders

Thomas Jefferson realized that government of, by, and for the people required a literate citizenry. He called for "the enlightenment of the people," which, in his time, meant literacy, to be achieved via compulsory, universal primary education. In the nineteenth century, secondary education became the rule, followed in the twentieth by a great expansion of college education. Even at this level, however, the focus has been on learning to use existing models, not discovering new ones.

In today's world, the ability to use models is no longer enough. To thrive in a world of perpetually changing ideas and beliefs, we need to cultivate our innate human talent for *building* models. This calls for a change in the orientation of education at every level as well as enhanced opportunities for education extending through adulthood. Lifelong learning will be the rule, not the exception, and a dignitarian society will make it accessible to all, regardless of one's ability to pay. New learning formats, which effectively challenge the presupposition that more learning means more schooling, are apt to become omnipresent as we move further into the digital age.

But can the elusive skills of innovation, discovery, and creativity that lie at the heart of model building be successfully taught? To borrow Jefferson's inclusive language, is the enlightenment of the people—in the modern sense of educating a society of model builders—a realistic goal?

In medieval Europe, it was primarily priests who could read and write; literacy was deemed beyond the reach of ordinary folk. Today, enlightenment—in the sense of having the capability for revelatory insights needed in model building—is likewise held by many to be an esoteric faculty gifted to or attainable by only a chosen few. To establish a dignitarian society irreversibly, we have to do for enlightenment what universal primary education did for literacy: demystify the process and teach it to all.

Demystifying Enlightenment—Jefferson Redux

Live your life as if there are no miracles and everything is a miracle.
—Albert Einstein

Although the experience of enlightenment has acquired a rarefied mystique in both East and West, the form relevant to twenty-first-century model builders is neither esoteric nor uncommon. In seeking to understand this phenomenon we can draw upon the inquiring traditions.

Scientific research culminates in the "eureka" of discovery. Artists describe their creative breakthroughs in remarkably similar language. Political transformation often originates in the emergence of a new personal identity, becoming the basis for a revised group consensus. (As the modern women's movement has taught us, "The personal is political.") Religious practices aim variously for emptiness, illumination, clarity, synthesis, self-realization, transcendence, or union with God.

In each of these arenas, protracted immersion in mundane details can lead to epiphanies. Although these may feel like bolts from the blue, they are usually preceded by a long period of drudgery. Typically we spend months, years, or even decades investigating something, pursuing a question, or applying ourselves to an endeavor. For what seems an eternity, we make one mistake after another, experience failure upon failure. Without this groundwork, breakthroughs rarely happen. It is only when we are steeped in the material and its contradictions—often feeling confused and hopeless—that resolution occurs in a revelatory insight wherein an old, collapsing model is superseded by a better one. Depending on the context, "better" can mean more useful, effective, accurate, comprehensive, beautiful, elegant, or loving. Convincing others that what we've come upon is indeed better may take longer still, sometimes even beyond our own lifetime.

From this perspective, the experience of enlightenment—whether in a scientific, artistic, political, or spiritual context—is seen as a movement of mind that lasts but an instant rather than a sublime state that, once attained, becomes our blissful abode forever. In the framework of model building, enlightenment is the exhilarating experience of a fresh perception breaking the stranglehold of habit. Czeslaw Milosz, the Polish Nobel laureate in literature, said this of narrative description: "[It] demands intense observation, so intense that the veil of everyday habit falls away and what we paid no attention to, because it struck us as so ordinary, is revealed as miraculous." The differences in enlightenment as experienced in various fields pale in comparison with the deep similarities common to them all—a sense of blinders having been removed, of clear sight at last, of ecstatic revelation.[14]

The experience of enlightenment can be thought of as a leap across a precipice from one foothold to another, except that it's unintentional and unpredictable. For a period after landing we may feel elated, but it's a mistake to confuse this afterglow with enlightenment itself. The latter is not the condition into which we have vaulted; rather, it is the leap that took us there.

That moments of enlightenment can't be anticipated accounts for part of our fascination with them, but it also makes the experience vulnerable to mystification. History has seen many claimants to the titles of sage, genius, maestro, saint, or master. Transfixed by such figures, mesmerized by the aura of celebrity and mystery that envelops them, we often fail to notice that, like ourselves, they are ordinary human beings. When they're not having an epiphany—which is most of the time—they're much the same as everyone else. What sets them apart is a readier ability to rise above habit and see things freshly, thereby opening themselves to multiple enlightenment experiences. Interestingly, virtually none of those who genuinely exhibit this talent lay claim to being enlightened. Albert Einstein poked fun at what he viewed as the popular misrepresentation of his abilities with the wry observation, "I am no Einstein." Innumerable saints have said as much. Fortunately, the reticence and humility of those who establish a capacity for recurrent enlightenment experiences do not prevent, and may even help, them impart this key talent to students and followers. Whether using it will result in a student hitting a first jackpot or the teacher hitting a second or third one—of that, alas, no one can be certain.

Students and seekers often collude in their own infantilization by maintaining habits of deference that lull them into believing that a creative breakthrough is something quite beyond them. Such dependent relationships with revered authority figures reflect a desire for a parent whose love is constant, whose wisdom is infallible, and on whom we can always rely. They may also come to serve as an excuse for not assuming responsibility ourselves: "How could I ever compete with the *Master*?" The best teachers, like the best parents, freely transmit their knowledge, skills, and passion for truth-seeking to their charges without leaving them starry-eyed. As with so many of the most precious gifts in life, the best we can do to thank such benefactors is to pass what we've learned from them on to someone else.

An experience of enlightenment may come while arranging a bouquet for the dinner table or painting one destined for the Louvre, in a never-repeated phrase spoken to a friend or one that will be quoted for centuries, during an ascent of Mt. Everest or a walk in the park. Some breakthroughs get the Nobel Prize, some an acknowledging nod from a companion or a stranger. Others still are met only with inner recognition. But all involve breaking a habit and provide us with a new way of beholding the outer world or our inner selves.

In religious traditions, teachers impart the most profound truths (often amounting to *metatruths*—that is, truths about truth-seeking itself, or truth-seeking strategies) to students through what is aptly called "transmission of mind." The phrase captures the transfer of model-building skills, regardless of the field of inquiry. There were times during my physics training when I felt I was experiencing a transmission of mind from my professor, John Wheeler, merely by hanging out with him and observing closely as he tackled problems. Sometimes he'd pass on something he attributed to one of his mentors, Niels Bohr. Transmissions of mind often have a lineage, but they include more grandmothers and schoolteachers than Nobel laureates.

In the twenty-first century, as more and more people realize their model-building potential, the capacity for, and experience of, enlightenment will spread throughout the world, much as reading and writing did in the twentieth.

DOCTORS ARE SEEN AS SOMEBODIES. WHAT SEPARATES THEM FROM
HEALERS IS THAT HEALERS BRIDGE THE GAP BETWEEN SOMEBODY AND
NOBODY BY FORMING A PARTNERSHIP WITH PATIENTS BASED ON EQUAL
DIGNITY. I BELIEVE THAT AFFIRMATION OF EVERYONE'S PERSONHOOD
IS A HEALING INTERACTION FOR PATIENT AND HEALER ALIKE.
—DR. JEFFREY RITTERMAN, KAISER PERMANENTE

The Evolving Doctor-Patient Relationship

RANKISM PERMEATES all the professions, and health care is no exception. Historically, medicine relied on the extreme difference in rank between physicians and patients to elicit trust, compliance, and hope during times of illness. But now, emboldened by knowledge gleaned from books, support groups, and the Internet, people are transforming themselves from docile patients into informed, engaged clients. Increasingly, patients come to the doctor's office with sophisticated questions and a desire to participate in decisions regarding their treatment. The era of the "MDeity" is passing into oblivion, and the traditional model of doctor-patient relationships is gradually being replaced with one of partnership.[1] In light of this historic shift, it's no surprise that recent studies suggest that apologies from doctors significantly reduce the incidence of malpractice lawsuits.[2]

Another example of patients' increasing desire to have a say in health matters is the hospice movement. By championing the idea of death with dignity, hospices have enabled people to retain as much responsibility for their end-of-life care as possible rather than surrender it wholesale to health care providers.

Rankism Among Health Professionals

In the larger fraternity of white coat providers, rankism manifests itself among practitioners holding different ranks. Doctors taking advantage of interns is a ubiquitous theme on hospital TV shows. Residents find themselves both recipients of and contributors to abusive situations, and nurses have legitimate complaints about their treatment by physicians. Within the nursing order—nurse practitioners, registered nurses, licensed volunteer nurses, and medical assistants—rankism also rears its ugly head. All of this takes its toll not only on caregivers, but ultimately on patients as well.

Relationships between practitioners of different medical modalities and orientations—allopathic, naturopathic, and the various schools of complementary and alternative medicine—are also infected with rankism. Certainly, when it comes to treatment, there are legitimate questions concerning effectiveness. But methodological standards often are not applied evenhandedly to the practices and cures advocated by different traditions. And organizations representing these traditions vie mightily with each other like medieval guilds to foster and maintain the demand for their own services rather than focusing objectively on what works best for patients.

Not surprisingly, the rankism that infects health care arises in part from the way in which its professionals are educated.[3] The seventy-two-hour shift for interns is a legendary horror story in point. Like other initiation or hazing rites, such exploitation is dangerous—in this case it adversely affects the health of the interns and increases the chance of their making medical mistakes.[4] In addition, these "ceremonies of degradation" perpetuate a rankist environment because they predispose young physicians to repeat the behavior once they've gained membership in the exclusive club that has been tormenting them. As the training of health care providers is stripped of traditional indignities, graduates will lose the desire to impose them on the next generation.

With the advent of managed care, doctors have also become increasingly vulnerable to bureaucratic rankism. In an e-mail dated July 8, 2005, a high-level administrator in the Office of Inspector General of the U.S. Department of Health and Human Services reported on what he hears from physicians working in health maintenance organizations:

> Doctors say they feel like nobodies because that's how the health care system treats them now. Many HMOs impose restrictions on how physicians provide patient care. For example, they are under pressure from management to see no fewer than a set number of patients each day, and limits are placed on how much time they can spend with each one. Doctors were trained to see themselves as healers, yet to a health administrator they are pieceworkers. However, recently the situation is beginning to change as a result of pressure from doctors and patients.

Another manifestation of rankism to which doctors are subjected is best understood as "reverse rankism." I've heard from a number of doctors that with the loss of their former godlike status, some patients try to turn the tables on them. Armed with a few tidbits they've picked up from the Internet, they attempt to pull rank on their doctors. A brief conversation clarifying the evolving doctor-patient relationship is usually all it takes to establish a healthier partnership.

The Health Benefits of Recognition

All these forms of rankism have counterparts within other hierarchical entities such as the academic, legal, and ecclesiastic professions, as well as business, the police, and the military. However, health care practitioners bear a double burden because they must deal not only with the rankism within their own hierarchy but also the casualties created by rankist abuse in all the others.

The rankism that pervades society is a serious threat to public health in much the same way that smoking is. This analogy can even be extended to "secondhand rankism"—namely, that resulting from passing a rankist insult along to someone of lower rank, sometimes referred to as the "kick-the-dog" phenomenon. The depredations to which the working poor are exposed take an unremarked toll that, over a lifetime, shows up as significantly enhanced morbidity and reduced life expectancy. A cover story in the *New York Times Magazine* makes the case that the ongoing stress experienced by those of low socioeconomic status in inner cities is a silent, unperceived killer.[5]

In an e-mail communication, Dr. Jeffrey Ritterman, who is chief cardiologist at the Kaiser Permanente HMO in Richmond, California, acknowledged this. Noting that his hospital serves a population of low socioeconomic status and great ethnic diversity, he observed: "Many of our patients suffer from nobody status, which deeply affects their health outcomes." That rankism is also a factor in determining *who* is afforded health care becomes especially clear in the aftermath of crises like Hurricane Katrina, which exhausted resources in New Orleans and along the Gulf Coast in 2005.

In ancient times, an excruciating form of execution was known as "death by a thousand cuts." Its modern counterpart is "death by a thousand indignities." As evidence of the adverse effects of rankism on public health mounts, health care professionals are going to feel honor bound to educate the public about the social costs of malrecognition. To deal with this public health menace we are going to have to purge rankism from all our social institutions in the same way that, led by a series of Surgeons General, we are curtailing public smoking.

Given the cumulative damage wrought by indignity, we should expect to see benefits to those who manage to shield themselves from it. A study by Dr. Donald Redelmeier of the University of Toronto suggests exactly that. He reports that Oscar winners live on average almost four years longer than other actors. For multiple Oscar winners, it's six years. Dr. Redelmeier argues that such success has a powerful influence on a person's health and longevity. He says, "Once you've got that statuette on your mantel, it's an uncontested sign of peer approval that nobody can take away from you. [Winning an Oscar] leaves you more resilient. Harsh reviews don't quite get under your skin. The normal stresses and strains of everyday life don't drag you down."[6]

Dr. Nancy Adler, director of the Center for Health and Community and professor of medical psychology at the University of California at San Francisco, says:

> Status is made up of many things—it's a matter of education, money, ethnicity, and gender. What we're learning is that in each of those areas, health is better the higher up you are.
>
> The issue for stress is not how many demands you have, but your sense that they are manageable. A demand that you have the resources to deal with—that you have some control over—can actually be invigorating. It's the difference between a challenge and a threat. Control goes up at each step up the social ladder and that usually works to diminish stress.[7]

Dr. Adler quotes Leonard Syme of the University of California's School of Public Health: "If you could only ask one question of a person, and you wanted to be able to predict what their state of health would be, it would be their social class."[8] Syme showed that it wasn't just that those of the highest status had a longer life span and better overall health than those at the bottom, but that health improved with each rung up the social hierarchy. It is important to recognize that higher social class doesn't just mean better health care. It also often means less exposure to rankism, which in turn means less need for health care.

In this vein, Michael Marmot, a professor of epidemiology and public health at University College London and author of *The Status Syndrome: How Social Standing Affects Our Health and Longevity*, writes:

> The higher your status in the social hierarchy the better your health and the longer you live.... A way to understand the link between status and health is to think of three fundamental human needs: health, autonomy, and opportunity for full social participation.... The lower

the social status, the less autonomy and the less social participation. Participation includes the positive feedback one receives from social recognition and being a valued member of society.[9]

Dignity: A Centerpiece of Health Care

This brief survey of the effects of rankism on health and the health care system suggests that any systemwide fix will need to make dignity its centerpiece. To be successful today, a health care model must proffer respect for patients, who are rebelling against their traditional infantilization; it must preserve the dignity of doctors and nurses, most of whom have chosen the profession out of a desire to serve; and finally, it must respect the indispensable role of administrators, who have the thankless task of managing a scarce but desperately needed resource.

Quite obviously, no society can regard itself as dignitarian if access to quality health care is limited to those with enough money to afford it. Equally obvious is that health care, like any resource, is limited in supply and must be rationed some way or other. Controlling access to it by the ability to pay might be justified when a resource is optional, but not when it is indispensable to life, liberty, and the pursuit of happiness. Clearly health care falls into that category, and accordingly, a dignitarian society will see to it that everyone can readily obtain both routine and specialized evaluation and treatment in the mode of their choice. The organization Search for Common Ground has put together a project involving leading national stakeholders reflecting a broad spectrum of interests and perspectives. Its goal is to identify consensus-based recommendations to provide health care coverage to "as many people as possible as quickly as possible." The idea is to develop widely supportable proposals among these "strange bedfellows" in the hope of breaking a decades-old gridlock on how to extend coverage to the uninsured.[10]

In conclusion, here is an example that illustrates both the bureaucratic obstacles to building a dignitarian health care system, and what a determined government official can do to offset the dependence of health on social status. In 1995, Thomas A. Purvis, an evaluator in the office of the Inspector General in the U.S. Department of Health and Human Services, became aware that only a small fraction of youth covered by Medicaid were actually making use of the dental services for which they were eligible. He conducted a study to find out why. His principal findings were:

1. Bureaucratic red tape and inadequate reimbursement were factors in why dentists did not seek business from low-income families. But these were not the only reasons.
2. Dentists were turning down young Medicaid patients and their families because they viewed them in a way that smacked of rankism. The dentists tended to stereotype all such patients as being uninformed about the importance of good dental care, disruptive in the waiting room, unreliable about keeping appointments, and disinclined to follow their recommendations regarding home care between visits.

As a result of Purvis's analysis, state and federal agencies began working together to disabuse the dental profession of its perception of Medicaid patients. In combination with raising the fees paid to dentists, this strategy resulted in a significant elevation in the percentage of children from low-income families served by the Medicaid-funded dental program.[11]

This story suggests that positive intervention by a service-oriented bureaucracy can offset the impact of rankism on health. But an October 2005 article in the *New York Times* indicates that, while some progress has been made, the same social status factors that were identified by Purvis ten years ago continue to limit the numbers of those eligible for Medicaid who are actually served by the program.[12]

Today, rankist barriers in health care are like the racist barriers in public accommodations that existed before the nation enacted the civil rights legislation of the 1960s. Until these barriers are removed, they will continue to do serious disservice to a large group of citizens.

THE SOCIAL CONTRACT IN A DIGNITARIAN SOCIETY 7

POVERTY IS THE NEW SLAVERY.
—REVEREND JIM WALLIS, *GOD'S POLITICS*

THE EXCLUSION OF one group of people or another has been the rule through most of history. Men without property could be denied the vote in revolutionary America. Quotas were placed on Jews in many universities and professions until the midtwentieth century. Women were denied the vote in many countries well into the last century, and still are in some. Likewise, the segregation of African Americans was widely sanctioned in the United States until the 1960s. At one time or another, most societies have rationalized relegating certain subgroups to second-class citizenship.

Institutional Rankism and a Permanent Underclass

As racism disadvantaged blacks and sexism restricted women, so rankism marginalizes the working poor, keeping them in their place while their low salaries effectively make goods and services available to society at subsidized prices. This process, whereby the most indigent Americans have become the benefactors of those better off, is vividly described by Barbara Ehrenreich in her book, *Nickel and Dimed.*[1] In *The Working Poor: Invisible in America,* author David Shipler depicts the less fortunate as disappearing into a "black hole" from which there is no exit.[2] As class membranes become ever less permeable, resignation, cynicism, and hostility mount.

Exposing the institutional rankism that consigns millions to an underclass is a Herculean political task, but the theoretical groundwork is already being laid. In addition to the volumes already mentioned, there is *Shortchanged: Life and Debt in the Fringe Economy,* by Howard Karger, which shows how the working poor and also many in the middle class become mired in a netherworld of high interest rates and ever-mounting debt.[3] Except for the absence of debtors' prisons today, their situation is redolent of nineteenth-century Dickensian England.

Some marginalized groups have managed to end their exclusion and win for themselves a measure of social justice. But many are still trapped in Nobodyland—often less because they bear traits that in the past were used to sanction discrimination than that they are mired in poverty. How can a dignity movement aimed at overcoming rankism provide a way out for the underclass?

The Myth of Meritocracy

The rank-based strategy of the movement to equalize dignity stands in sharp contrast to the class-based Marxist strategy committed to equalizing wealth. As practiced, communism created a rankist elite that usurped riches and power for itself. In contrast, a dignitarian society aims to eliminate the "dignity gaps" created and perpetuated by rankism.

Today the working poor are typically devoid of savings and utterly dependent on regular weekly wages. A medical emergency, the loss of a job, even a car repair can force them—including many in the middle class—into an untenable level of credit card debt or even homelessness. Increasingly, low social rank, or class, poses an all but impassable barrier to social mobility. Accepting such an arrangement is tantamount to giving up on democracy's promise of liberty and justice for all. To the extent that social mobility is a myth, so is meritocracy.

One does not need as much money or as high an income as one's neighbors or co-workers to live a life of dignity. But one must be free to compete on equal terms with those who currently hold higher rank. To vie for rank on a level playing field and lose is neither cause for, nor is it experienced as, indignity. But to be denied even the chance to do so is a preemptory form of exclusion. Few, if any, meritocracies, though they offer more social mobility than the aristocracies of past centuries, qualify as dignitarian.

People who have money know that it's the foundation on which their personal freedom rests. Even modest savings allow them to leave a job that ill suits them, opt out of a bad school, or see a dentist or doctor. While a dignitarian society would not compensate everyone equally, everyone would be paid enough to afford such choices.

Where would the money come from? The price increases that paying a living wage to all would necessitate would ultimately be borne by consumers, who, of course, include the working poor themselves. But under the present system, their undercompensated labor functions as a hidden subsidy to everyone. As long as a majority of voters are comfortable with that, it will continue. But when awareness dawns that "poverty is the new slavery," growing numbers of people are likely to become intolerant of this situation.

I was surprised when, in 1971, a student at Oberlin College petitioned the investment committee of the school's board of trustees to divest itself of its stock in companies that operated in apartheid South Africa.[4] But within a few years, a worldwide divestiture movement was putting pressure on that country to abandon its policy of apartheid.

Today, working conditions in the overseas plants of global corporations are coming under similar scrutiny. It's not much of a stretch to imagine this kind of awareness being focused on the plight of the "nickel and dimed" in the United States. Once it is widely understood that the working poor are involuntary benefactors of society, acceptance of this injustice could change just as the world's tolerance for apartheid did. Feeling indebted to people who are less well off is not something that many are comfortable with.

In addition to having an equitable system of compensation, a dignitarian society would be one in which most people owned property. On the face of it, this would seem to require some redistribution of assets, and historically this has led to social unrest if not violence. But if instead of attempting any kind of wholesale reallocation of wealth we limit ourselves to tax policies that gradually effect a marginal shift, we may be able to chart a nonviolent democratic path to a society in which everyone has an honest chance to realize the proverbial American dream.

One thing is certain: inclusion works, exclusion doesn't. Equal opportunity is the path to inclusion while rankism is an instrument of exclusion. Systematically removing the rankist barriers that imprison the underclass is the counterpart of removing the segregationist laws that for so long kept people of color out of the mainstream.

Models of "Democratic Capitalism"

Following in the footsteps of Thomas Paine, who was among the first to advocate that society had an obligation to address material inequality and poverty through a system of public welfare, many political thinkers have suggested mechanisms of economic inclusion. The following paragraphs present several such possibilities. But more important than the details of any particular plan is the commitment to finding and implementing one. As Paine argued in *Agrarian Justice*, written in 1797, societies in which it is virtually impossible to escape from poverty forfeit not only social cohesiveness but also moral leadership.

> It is wrong to say God made both *rich* and *poor*. He made only *male* and *female*; and He gave them the earth for their inheritance.
>
> Payments [from the national fund are to] be made to every person, rich or poor. It is best to make it so, to prevent invidious distinctions. ... [Those who] do not choose to receive it can throw it into the common fund.[5]

In his forthcoming book *Re-Birth of a Nation: American Identity and the Culture Wars*, Richard Baldwin gives new impetus to the idea that political independence has to be rooted in economic independence. Baldwin's proposal, which incorporates aspects of several other plans, calls for the establishment of Individual Capital Endowments (ICEs) for the young. In his vision, every child is taught money management—perhaps even to run a model business—as part of primary and secondary school education. (Finally, a compelling reason to learn arithmetic!) On reaching adulthood at age eighteen, everyone is provided with enough capital resources to pay for a college education or start a business and to make a down payment on a home. Baldwin's basic thesis is that the way to end de facto segregation under which the poor suffer is to train all young people to be capitalists.

Baldwin's ICEs are modeled on Michael Sherraden's Individual Development Accounts (IDAs), which in turn are based on the now ubiquitous IRAs. IDAs grow over time with the goal of ensuring that every household has a stake in society and a cushion against unemployment or illness. In the same spirit, Bruce Ackerman and Ann Alstott, in their book *The Stakeholder Society,* have proposed that as Americans reach adulthood they receive a onetime grant of $80,000 financed by a tax on the nation's accumulated assets.[6]

All these plans give expression to the dignitarian principle that everyone's success is dependent on contributions from untold others and that accordingly, everyone is obligated to contribute to a fair starting point for everyone else. This idea is analogous to the principle of revenue sharing in professional sports, which levels the playing field by offsetting the advantages that accrue to wealthier teams.

The major issue that any such program must confront is funding. I include an excerpt from Richard Baldwin's proposal not because it's *the* answer (there cannot be *any* definitive answer absent a dignitarian process), but rather to suggest that economically feasible solutions do exist and to start a conversation that can lead to one that is politically acceptable. Baldwin calls his plan *democratic capitalism.*

> What distinguished America as a very young nation was the almost universal possession of capital assets by immigrants of European origin. The primary domestic function of the federal government before the Civil War was to provide sufficient capital, in the form of land, to underwrite the economic independence of families. Subsequent

examples of governmental transfer of capital to individuals are the Homestead Act and the GI Bill.

A modern proposal along these lines is Individual Capital Endowments, which would be allotted to each child at birth. A reasonable sum might be the cost of tuition for a four-year postsecondary education at a state university plus the equivalent of a 10 percent down payment on a median-priced home. Under present conditions, that would require about $200 billion annually—a substantial investment but manageable for the American economy.

One source of funding for the program would be estate taxes, which at current levels provide about $30 billion a year, 15 percent of the total needed. Estate taxes are out of fashion but if we seriously want to create a dignitarian society, we need to reconsider them. No matter how brilliant and hard-working an individual effort is, capital accumulation is always to some degree a public creation built in part on contributions from others. It is therefore appropriate that a portion of it be shared with society. This applies to any accumulation of assets, no matter how large or small. In particular, there is no reason that a progressive reform of the estate tax could not yield 25 percent of the annual funding needed for [Individual] Capital Endowments.

Approximately 50 percent could come from nontax dollars. Every corporation with publicly traded stock would annually contribute 1 percent of its total outstanding shares at the end of the prior year. The final 25 percent would come from taxes levied on privately held productive capital assets such as closely held companies and real estate—a "wealth tax" rather like that proposed in Ackerman and Alstott's *The Stakeholder Society.*

This mode of financing the program would produce a gradual, systematic, and broadly based redistribution of assets without punitive taxation or serious disruption of financial markets. Over a period of 20 to 30 years, the cumulative shift of assets would reach socially significant proportions.

The resources involved would be held initially by a National Endowment Mutual Fund—a quasi-public corporation similar to

Fannie Mae. The fund would function like TIAA-CREF, dividing its assets into mutual funds of diversified investments.

Endowment funds would not be available to parents and would become fully vested when a person reached the age of 30. Assets held by any individual who dies before the full vesting would be returned to the general pool to help finance the following year's new endowments.

The great promise of a "democratic capitalism" is its potential to heal a society riven with dignity gaps. A hand-to-mouth existence is as incompatible with dignity as is lack of access to health care and education. Without a living wage the American dream is a mirage. An inclusive economics affirms every citizen's inherent dignity.[7]

Equal opportunity is sometimes confused with equal outcomes. Obviously, it is no such thing. In a fair race, all the runners at the starting line have an equal opportunity to win, but only one of them gets the gold medal. However, this is all right. Our dignity does not depend on winning or even tying. It depends on doing our best in a fair contest and not facing humiliation or degradation if we lose. It depends on having an honest chance and then finding a niche from which we can contribute something commensurate with our particular talents and abilities. Dignity also depends on being acknowledged for making this contribution and on being compensated well enough so that we (and our dependents) can continue to play the game.

Besting others in a contest that has been fixed may bring us loot or glory but it carries no lasting satisfaction. Instead, it sows doubts about our achievement that leave us feeling insecure and guilty. Heaven forbid that we should lose a later competition and expose ourselves to the indignities now visited upon those we've vanquished in an unfair match! A dignitarian society promises what we all really need: not necessarily a win, but an honest chance at winning that brings out the best in us.

Given the certainty that some fraction of the population will suffer failure and even catastrophe, plans like Baldwin's do not permit the dismantling of the social safety net. But as rankism is eliminated and equal opportunity becomes a reality, we can expect welfare programs to diminish in scope and size. Funds spent ensuring a fair chance for everyone are more productive than funds spent trying to correct the effects of chronic malrecognition.

Second-class citizenship is incompatible with dignity—not only the dignity of those consigned to it, but the collective dignity of the society that tolerates the discrimination. Creating pathways out of poverty is essential to the integrity of any dignity movement. A dignitarian society will finally deliver on Jefferson's promise that "all are created equal."[8]

THE POLITICS
OF DIGNITY 8

DEMOCRACY IS THE WORST FORM OF GOVERNMENT,
EXCEPT FOR ALL THE OTHERS THAT HAVE BEEN TRIED.
—WINSTON CHURCHILL

ALL THE ILLS OF DEMOCRACY CAN BE CURED BY MORE DEMOCRACY.
—ALFRED E. SMITH, FORMER GOVERNOR OF NEW YORK

THE PRICE OF LIBERTY IS SOMETHING MORE THAN
ETERNAL VIGILANCE. . . . WE CAN SAVE THE RIGHTS WE HAVE
INHERITED FROM OUR FATHERS ONLY BY WINNING
NEW ONES TO BEQUEATH OUR CHILDREN.
—HENRY DEMAREST LLOYD, AMERICAN JOURNALIST AND REFORMER

THE PREVIOUS CHAPTERS have discussed rankism in our social institutions and what can be done to curtail it. Here we address rankism in our civic institutions. What would politics look like if it were conducted in a dignitarian manner? What is the relationship between citizens and their leaders in a dignitarian government? Must partisan politics lead to ideological extremes or is there common ground that both conservatives and progressives can inhabit and thereupon work out their differences?

Before people take seriously the possibility of building dignitarian political institutions, they need an answer to a question I'm asked at every talk I give:

Is Rankism Human Nature?

In general, it's a rule of nature to pick on the weak—a strategy that minimizes the chance of retaliation. Since human beings are not unlike other species in this regard, it's natural to conclude that rankism is human nature and that's the whole story. But it's not. Yes, human beings are predators. But we're also changing rapidly. Numerous observers have made the case that we're now in the final phase of an epochal transition from predatory behavior to cooperative conduct.[1]

Rankism is dominating, sometimes predatory, behavior, but it is not indelibly etched into our brains. In fact, the opposite is the case. The record shows that over the course of time, the weak have periodically rebelled against oppression and domination, often with striking success. Although this is usually the culmination of a long and harrowing process, human beings have repeatedly shown themselves capable of imposing limits on the authority of strongmen. Famous instances include the English barons at Runnymede who forced King John to sign the Magna Carta in 1215, the birth of parliaments limiting the absolute powers of sovereigns, colonials expelling their imperialist masters, and in the twentieth century, the global spread of democracy and the defeat or collapse of dictatorships that challenged it.

We have also witnessed the rise of organized labor and other mass movements, such as those for civil and women's rights, in response to discrimination and exploitation by a dominant group. It was long maintained that racism and sexism are indelible parts of human nature, but with every passing decade this belief becomes more indefensible. So while it must be acknowledged that we do have predatory tendencies, it's also clear that we're quite capable of reining them in and that this latter-day trend seems likely to prevail as our species matures.

At every point in our social evolution, power rules. Usually it's imminent and in your face—the police, the army—but every now and then what prevails is a novel combination of lesser forces that, through collaboration, first trump and then tame the existing authority. Sometimes all it takes to persuade those in charge to back down is to convince them that should things actually come to a fight, they will lose. Abuses of power persist until the individuals or institutions perpetrating them realize that they are facing a greater force. That force need not be, and usually is not, entirely material. As Gandhi, Martin Luther King, Jr., and Nelson Mandela proved, an important part of that force can be the moral might of an aroused citizenry.

In any case, once the opposition coalesces the rankist perpetrators either mend their ways or end up being ousted from their privileged positions. The long-term trend of this evolutionary process is the discovery of increasingly effective forms of cooperation that outperform, outproduce, and finally supplant abusive authoritarianism. Examples of this dynamic can be found in the myriad autocracies that have yielded to democracies and in the replacement of companies fueled by fear and humiliation with businesses providing work environments that protect people's dignity so that everyone, custodian and stockholder alike, reaps the benefits.

It is a goal of this book to make the principles of a dignitarian society palpable enough so the very thought of doing something that subjects others to indignity will provoke the countervailing realization that such a course would, in the longer term, prove self-defeating if not suicidal. In addition to confronting the abuses that remain in our civic arena and social institutions, we must identify and eliminate those that occur between sovereign states, democratic or not, in the largely ungoverned realm of international affairs.

The DNA of Democracy: Watchdog Processes

Democracy is a strategy to combat the truth expressed in Lord Acton's oft-quoted dictum, "Power tends to corrupt and absolute power corrupts absolutely." It's the best model of governance we have for ensuring that officials do not misuse their station to the detriment of those they are supposed to serve.

The DNA of democracy consists of watchdog procedures through which we monitor our officials' actions and systems of accountability that circumscribe their prerogatives. Instead of assuming that authority figures will consistently respect human dignity, democracy assumes the opposite: that they will be tempted to place their personal interests ahead of the public's, and that if this causes the citizens indignity—well, that's just too bad. To prevent such self-serving lapses, we erect a system of constant "reminders," such as multiple political parties, elections, checks and balances including an independent judiciary, free media—all the institutions of democratic civil life—to hold their feet to the fire.

Woody Allen joked that relationships are like sharks: they either keep moving or they die. Democracy is a relationship between those in positions of authority and the citizenry, and if we're not continually saving it, we're losing it. The reason for this is that new forms of power are constantly emerging and democracy has to keep pace with them to guard against potential creeping transgressions—that is, new instances of rankism. One example of this is the way television has transformed the political process, giving an advantage to candidates with the financial resources to purchase the most broadcast time. This makes it easier for the wealthy to acquire and wield power, and as many commentators have pointed out, it moves nations away from democracy toward plutocracy.[2] In response, some European governments are striving to reduce the role of money in politics by attempting to equalize what candidates spend on media campaigns.

But television has also had another effect on politics, one that serves the weak. Like the printing press before it and the Internet later, television informs, and insofar as it's accurate, information is empowering. Although technological innovations may at first benefit the authorities, who are usually quicker to exploit them, citizens eventually get their hands on new advances and over time, this strengthens their position vis-à-vis those in charge.

Television has made of the world a global village in which everyone knows how the other half lives. The Internet, cell phones, and text messaging shift power away from the governors toward the governed. The growing use of blogs on the Internet is another example of how technological innovations bring change to government, in this case by amplifying the voices of citizens and weakening the traditional media's control over the news. The Internet is a democratizing tool that offers vast numbers of people affordable ways to publish, make videos, produce music—in short, to communicate, contribute, and gain recognition. As such it is a dignitarian bulwark against rankism.

Democracy evolves as a majority of citizens realize that eliminating identified forms of rankism benefits society as a whole. A government's legitimacy rests on its capability and willingness to put the interests of the citizenry as a whole over those of any subgroup, no matter how powerful. Decisions that favor an elite rather than the country as a whole are quite literally unpatriotic.

Navigating the Ship of State

The partisan divide into right and left, conservative and liberal, stems from the ongoing and unavoidable choice facing all societies over how much authority to vest in rank. The right has traditionally been the party that defends the authority and prerogatives of powerholders, the left the party that limits them. These identifications can reverse, however, depending on which party is in charge. When the left overthrew the Czar and took over during the Russian Revolution of 1917, it quickly abolished all limits on governmental power.

Since both right and left orientations have a vital role in good management, it's not surprising that democratic electorates tilt first one way and then the other. They are like the captain of a ship who makes a continual series of course corrections, to starboard and port, in order to avoid beaching the ship (of state) on the shoals (of extremism).

This simple model of left-right complementarity is complicated by the existence of multiple levels of authority: national, regional or state, municipal, and individual. Both the left and the right may try to use the power of one level of government to weaken or strengthen that held at other levels or by certain people. Examples include progressive support for, and conservative opposition to, national civil rights legislation during the segregationist era and the present-day federal protection of abortion rights. Another current example, in which the attitude of left and right toward federal power is reversed, is conservative support for, and progressive opposition to, a constitutional amendment barring gay marriage. Generally, conservatives view governmental regulation and taxation as restrictions upon individual authority and autonomy and thus oppose them, whereas those on the left see these functions of government as fairly distributive of power and are more willing to support them.

Which party fulfills the progressive or conservative role is secondary compared to the overarching need to maintain social and political stability. A society that doesn't trust anyone with authority loses its ability to coordinate and execute complicated tasks in a timely fashion. Systems of governance that cannot "stop people talking," to use Clement Attlee's phrase cited in chapter 3, are vulnerable to what the women's movement in the 1960s called the "tyranny of structurelessness," which groups that govern by consensus will recognize as the interminable, indecisive meeting. On the other hand, a society that doesn't limit the power of its rulers (such as in the USSR and Nazi Germany) will find individual initiative stifled and liberty eroded. In this case, the threat is the tyranny of conformity.

What's imperative for civic stability and civil governance is that both upholding and circumscribing the power vested in rank have earnest advocates and that partisans be aware of and have some appreciation for the validity of the role played by their opponents. This duality is so important that even in one-party systems dedicated to some ideological principle, the divide between conservatives and liberals soon reappears in the form of "hard-liners" and "democratizers."

Navigating the ship of state between right and left reflects the need to avoid absolutism and anarchy, either of which can be the undoing of a government and a people. Systems of governance that lack such a steering mechanism are prone to self-destruct. Without its opposite number to serve as a counterweight, either party, unrestrained, will eventually run a nation aground. To paraphrase an unknown pundit, we have lunatic fringes so we know how far *not* to go.

An individual's political orientation is influenced by his or her own personal relationship to rank. For a variety of reasons—psychological and political, and, recent studies hint, even genetic[3]—some tilt conservative, and an approximately equal number tilt liberal. As Gilbert and Sullivan put it in their play *Iolanthe:*

I often think it's comical
How nature always does contrive
That every boy and every gal,
That's born into the world alive,
Is either a little Liberal,
Or else a little Conservative!

One determinant of personal political orientation can be compensatory: we may give our support to the party whose predilection we wish to strengthen within ourselves. Thus, the people who fear their own indiscipline may champion the party of law and order and leave telltale hints of their underlying motives by expressing excessive disdain for liberals, whom they perceive as libertines. And those who seek to dispel guilt for a history of domination or prejudice may do so by becoming proselytizing champions of the weak, thereby expiating their sins and gaining a sense of moral purity.

Another factor in party preference is that each of us carries within, to different degrees and at different times, a sense of being both a somebody and a nobody. Those who identify themselves with their inner nobody are more apt to sympathize with those whom society casts as underdogs or second-class citizens. Contrariwise, those who align themselves with their inner somebody are more apt to support the "law and order" party.

Regardless of political orientation, aversion to abuses of power can blind partisans to rank's legitimate functions. Likewise, excessive loyalty to powerholders can turn partisans into apologists for rank's misuse.[4]

Tracing peoples' political orientation to their relationship to authority helps explain why political argument is so rarely persuasive. A good deal of partisan dispute stems from our gut feelings about whether increasing or decreasing the power of officeholders, especially as it may bear on a current issue in which we ourselves stand to gain or lose, is the greater threat. Once that choice has been made, the "facts" can usually be spun to support it, and reciting them to someone in the other camp has little effect.

A Dignitarian Model of Politics

To sum up, fair and effective government requires balancing the need for some centralization of power with concern about its proper use. That in turn requires a political model in which both parties acknowledge the legitimate functions of power and are conscientious about limiting it to the proper sphere. In the dignitarian model, tension between liberals and conservatives is regarded as a natural part of working out the appropriate use of authority in a given situation. Instead of being locked in stalemate, the parties engage, without fear or malice, in an open process of give-and-take until a common understanding is reached. As rankism, like racism, falls into disrepute, the partisan insults, put-downs, and smears we have become accustomed to will find less favor with the electorate. Sneering at opposing views, contempt for nonbelievers, and personal attacks will all backfire, discrediting the purveyors and not their targets. There is no reason to expect dignitarian politics to be less argumentative, but there's every reason to believe it will be more civil.

The message of detachment common in Eastern religions provides a useful antidote to the rancor and self-righteousness of partisan politics. It encourages us to witness and acknowledge our reactions to a situation and see them as part of a larger picture. Activism is not conceived of as directed against an evil foe, but rather as part of a dynamic in which one's opponents also have a valid, if perhaps misguided, role. Detached activists, while putting their strongest case forward, take pains to protect the dignity of their adversaries in what is, after all, a struggle to identify and expose whatever specific ignorance is sustaining the conflict. If you lose sight of the dignity of your adversaries, it's a sign that you're intoxicated by your own ideology. According to a Mayan saying: *Tu eres me otro yo (You are my other self)*.[5]

A dignitarian politics, while allowing for partisanship, would be inhospitable to the ideological extremism and dysfunctional incivility that undermine many modern democracies. The most effective thing one side can do to win the cooperation of the other is to discover what it is that's right about the opponent's position. Once a party to a conflict feels that some kernel of truth it defends has been appreciated by the other side and incorporated into a broader model—one that transcends the starting positions of both adversaries—it becomes easier for that party to cooperate. The day often goes to the side that takes the lead in figuring out a way for its opponents to hold their heads high while both sides abandon some of what they've been fighting for. Dignitarian politics is not so much nonpartisan as it is *transpartisan*.[6]

Confronting Bureaucratic Rankism

Rankism is *the* malady of bureaucracy. Regardless of state ideology, when bureaucrats put their interests above that of the public they're meant to serve, trust is eroded. Bureaucratic rankism is an equal opportunity disease afflicting communists and capitalists, fascists and democrats, liberals and conservatives alike.

But despite its endemic nature, rankism can indeed be overcome, one step at a time. Not that there aren't good grounds for cynicism. The rankist dysfunction that plagued FBI operations prior to the terrorist attacks of 9/11 has been identified by numerous investigative bodies. In hindsight, the success of the attacks was widely attributed to the rankist culture of law enforcement and intelligence agencies. The consensus is that on that fateful day America paid a tragic price for deeply ingrained habits that caused the FBI and CIA to put their institutional interests ahead of public safety.

In contrast to these high-profile instances of bureaucratic rankism are success stories that exemplify the opposite. Perhaps the most noteworthy recent example of overcoming the rankism of U.S. government officials is the Watergate scandal. A less publicized, closer-to-home example that directly affects every American taxpayer involves the Internal Revenue Service.

In 1997, during hearings of the Senate Finance Committee, it came to light that IRS agents and auditors were using the power of the agency to harass political dissidents, various religious groups, and certain other citizens by subjecting them to punitive audits. A whistle-blower named Shelley Davis, former historian for the IRS, described the "intransigence, arrogance, and abusive patterns of behavior that [are] common inside . . . the IRS" in her book *Unbridled Power: Inside the Secret Culture of the IRS*. In testimony to the committee she described the agency's Special Services Staff as a secret, cloistered unit of list-keepers. Anyone it considered "of questionable character," as determined from newspaper articles and their FBI files, was targeted for auditing even if they had no known tax problems.[7]

In this case the system of checks and balances worked as the Founding Fathers envisaged and the rankist agency practices at issue were identified and largely eliminated. As a result of the congressional hearings, the discretion of individual agents was removed from the equation. Rather than allowing them to target people based on their own opinions, a system was instituted that flagged returns for audit by computers programmed to pick up patterns of probable underpayment. This new arrangement eliminated personal discretion from the audit selection process and has gone a long way towards curbing abusive IRS power and quelling public concerns about it.

In a dignitarian culture, where the burden of proof is on alleged perpetrators instead of alleged victims, successes like this one shouldn't be hard to come by.

Seeking Common Ground

Imagine that a dignitarian approach to politics has taken hold. Parties of the left and the right continue to vie with each other for votes, but candidates who demonize their opponents are themselves discredited. Rather than being diverted by such sideshows, voters focus on whether their representatives are providing solutions that respect and protect their dignity.

In broad terms, what ideas and programs would we expect a legislature charged with overcoming rankism to come up with? Before giving an answer to this question, I want to acknowledge that this is only *my* answer—the kind of legislation I personally would wish my congressional representatives to enact to safeguard my dignity and that of my family. While it's tempting to guess at what others would want, that would be contrary to the letter and spirit of the dignitarian process. (Many of the following issues have been discussed in greater depth in earlier chapters.)

- ▶ *Dignity security,* not job security. This would provide a fair chance to compete for any job for which I have the specified qualifications, and transitional support if I should need to find a new one.
- ▶ Compensation for my labor that enables me and my dependents to live with dignity.
- ▶ Access to quality education for my family members regardless of our financial circumstances.
- ▶ Affordable basic and specialized health care for me and my dependents.
- ▶ A system for funding campaigns that enjoins lawmakers to put the public's interests above special interests. Incumbents should be barred from using the power inherent in their position to gain an unfair advantage over challengers.
- ▶ Protection of my privacy and autonomy against unwarranted intrusion from my fellow citizens or the government.
- ▶ An equitable tax policy. Obviously, everything depends on the interpretation of equitable. The word acquires a functional meaning through a national dignitarian dialogue. What we agree to be fair is fair, until we change our minds. Periodic renegotiation occurs in the form of a democratic political process that gives electoral weight to the interests of every citizen, with no exceptions.
- ▶ A national defense that deters would-be aggressors and defeats them if they mount an attack, along with international policies that avoid giving the kind of offense to others that incites their revenge.
- ▶ Participation in global agreements that foster international security and environmental sustainability.

More important than any of these particulars is to elect candidates who are committed in general to searching for models that protect the dignity of all.

How will all this be attained? Unfortunately, there is no quick way—any more than there was a way during the era of racial segregation to vote enough enlightened legislators into office to pass civil rights legislation. The process will take time.

And we shouldn't expect our political representatives to be more dignitarian than we are. If we ourselves presume ideological or moral superiority, our politicians will simply mirror one or another brand of it back to us in an ongoing attempt to find favor with a majority of voters. The result will be more of the same—unending, uncivil stalemate and stagnation.

To elect politicians who will build a dignitarian society requires the creation of a dignitarian culture. As this culture takes hold, our politicians will find it increasingly difficult, and ultimately impossible, to deny us dignitarian governance. Such a society will not come to us as a gift. It will come as we earn it—by personifying its values and demanding the same from our leaders.

The following chapter begins to examine how we can establish a dignitarian perspective and sketches out what the emerging dignitarian cultural consensus will look like.

A Culture of Dignity 9

THE PUBLIC . . . DEMANDS CERTAINTIES.
. . . BUT THERE ARE NO CERTAINTIES.
—H. L. MENCKEN, AMERICAN WRITER

KNOW YOU WHAT IT IS TO BE A CHILD?
. . . IT IS TO BELIEVE IN BELIEF.
—FRANCIS THOMPSON, BRITISH POET

THE INVESTIGATOR SHOULD HAVE A ROBUST
FAITH—AND YET NOT BELIEVE.
—CLAUDE BERNARD, FRENCH PHYSIOLOGIST

WHEN WE HEAR the word *fundamentalist* today, we tend to think of Christians, Jews, Muslims, or others who are rigid in their faith. Images of zealous evangelists, self-righteous proselytizers, and fanatics leap to mind.

But I use the word more broadly to refer to any true believers and even to that part of ourselves that might be closed-minded about one thing or another. By generalizing in this way, we include those who dismiss anything contrary to their particular absolutist views, whether religious, scientific, artistic, or ideological. Such a stance is the antithesis of the model-building perspective.

Can a fundamentalist thus construed be dignitarian? Or is it in the very nature of fundamentalism not only to presume the superiority of its doctrine but also to try to impose it on others?

Fundamentalism and the Dignitarian Perspective

Though the stereotype is that all fundamentalists are intolerant zealots, there are people who call themselves fundamentalists who hold that their beliefs are for themselves only and who make no effort to convert anyone else. They are not haughty, nor do they harm others merely by holding fast to their doctrines. It may be that the fixity of their beliefs limits them by keeping them from availing themselves of advances in scientific, political, or religious thought. But so long as they do not insist on converting others, they cannot be accused of rankism. If they secretly think of themselves as having a superior worldview—well, they're hardly alone in that regard.

On the other hand, if people assume the mantle of higher authority and presume to instruct others, then they are misappropriating rank, and that's rankism. Fundamentalism of this imperious bent comes in a variety of flavors: moral righteousness, technological arrogance, intellectual condescension, and artistic snobbery, to name a few. It tends to be magisterial, elitist, strident, domineering, supercilious, and overbearing.

In a dignitarian world, fundamentalists have to compete with all comers on an equal footing. Claims to represent higher authority are not given special credence and do not exempt a doctrine from scrutiny. Infallibility is out; questioning authority is not only permitted but encouraged. The one thing dignitarian tolerance does not extend to is intolerance—that is, to those who would resort to coercion to achieve their own agenda.

Chapter 1 presented a range of examples of fundamentalism: the traditional Confucianism that protected the rapist in rural China; the mantle of infallibility assumed by NASA officials who overruled the engineers on *Challenger;* the "commissars" on the Nuclear Regulatory Commission who arbitrarily substituted their own judgment for that of hands-on operators at Three Mile Island. In addition, there are fundamentalists of every faith who would impose their beliefs on others and revile those who disagree with them.

When scientists look down their noses at religious fundamentalists, they are as guilty of rankism as the targets of their disdain. It's true that most religious fundamentalists, much like cocksure ideologues and smug scientists, do close their minds, but a person has a right to do this. Almost all people have some compartmentalized beliefs that they exempt from questioning, and in that sense there is at least some of the fundamentalist in everyone. As we all know, though, the parts of us that are closed are unlikely to be opened by derision and contempt.

When adherents to any fundamentalist creed demonize dissenters as immoral or evil, they're treading a path that leads to dehumanization, oppression, and in the extreme, even to genocide. When nonbelievers put fundamentalists down as naïve and ignorant, they are taking the first step down that same treacherous path.

The problem is compounded by the fact that even when both parties agree to let the evidence settle the matter, there can be disagreement as to what constitutes evidence. One group might insist that anything in the Bible is ipso facto evidence, whereas the other might insist on substantiating biblical assertions with accepted scientific procedures. The only way to settle an impasse like this—aside from one side backing down—is to build a "metamodel" that reconciles the antagonists' views on basic methodological issues. As rankism is ruled out, believers and nonbelievers can narrow the scope of their disagreements and simply agree to disagree on what remains.

Ideology and the Dignitarian Perspective

As noted above, there's a little bit of the fundamentalist in almost everyone. It is in defense of that bit of "sacred," unquestioned terrain that we are most likely to inflict indignity on others. Becoming aware of these tendencies in ourselves is an essential part of creating a dignitarian environment. Inhabiting a post-fundamentalist world will not be easy. It requires breaking our dependency on "intoxicating certitudes," as it were, and finding our footing without recourse to absolutes.

When our models can't change, behavior patterns become frozen, including abusive and unjust ones. Thus, our attitude about the evolution of models—the degree of inner freedom we feel toward allowing this process to unfold—has important consequences for attempts to make relationships and institutions dignitarian.

One reason it can be so hard for us to accept the notion of changing models is that they are composed of interlocking sets of fondly held beliefs—and nothing dies harder than a cherished opinion. Many people are so identified with their beliefs that they react to the idea of revising them as they would to the prospect of losing an arm or a leg. Institutions are less flexible still. Fighting to defend our ideas often feels tantamount to fighting for our lives.

Avoiding the violence this breeds requires that we learn to hold beliefs not as unvarying absolutes but rather as working assumptions that, taken together, function as a pragmatic model. As we've seen, this is how natural scientists hold their theories. The same is true of artists and their sketches, cooks and their recipes, or dancers and their movements. Indeed, it is how people from every walk of life who are really good at what they do conduct themselves. What the public sees is the finished product. But typically, this has been arrived at through a great deal of improvisation and experimentation.

Creative people in every line of endeavor adopt beliefs provisionally for their usefulness and elegance and freely consider new ones as they present themselves to see if they are improvements over those currently held. As museum curator Kirk Varnedoe said: "Modern art writ large presents one cultural expression of a larger political gamble on the human possibility of living in change and without absolutes."[1] In a dignitarian world we'll hold beliefs not unto death, but until we find more accurate, comprehensive, useful replacements that prove their worth by enabling us to make more precise predictions, better pies, or more beautiful dances or paintings. Welcome to the post-fundamentalist era!

Detachment from our beliefs does not imply indifference, let alone resignation. The instinct to defend our beliefs strenuously does serve a higher purpose. Usually disagreements have a legitimate basis and the only way to advance toward a better model is to advocate for our views as effectively as we can while others do the same for theirs. We fail to serve the search for an improved model if we don't mount the strongest possible defense of our ideas. Each of us helps discover the new model by holding out until our individual perspective can be absorbed into a broader public synthesis stripped of personal idiosyncrasies.

This idea—the duty to advocate for our beliefs to the best of our ability—is one of the main themes in the Hindu holy book, the *Bhagavad Gita*. In a key passage, Lord Krishna counsels Prince Arjuna to fight his current foes, relatives, and those who were formerly allies—impersonally, dispassionately, and unreservedly.

The adversarial method, while intense, need not be personally antagonistic, even in those especially awkward situations in which we know our opponents intimately. That is the essence of dignitarianism. Once we accept the inherent inconstancy of beliefs, it's easier to entertain ones that differ from our own. From there, it's but a small step to recognizing the individuals who hold opposing views as worthy opponents and treating them with dignity. If it's our own case that crumbles in the end, we can simply admit our error and join in welcoming the discovery of something new and better. When our beliefs go to battle and lose, we ourselves live to argue another day, just as lawyers do when a judgment goes against one of their clients. Certain models turn out to be of limited validity, but this brings no shame upon their architects or advocates.

Not infrequently, we sense our own mistakes at about the same time others do. Why is it so difficult to admit such an awareness publicly? It's because we fear that admitting to imperfection or error will subject us to indignity, if not outright rejection. But this overlooks the fact that people ultimately love and respect each other not as perfect beings but as fallible human creatures whose very essence is the capacity for change.

It's in our own interest to admit a mistake once discovered because our own creativity and development are crippled if we don't. It need not damage us to be wrong, but it's debilitating to compound things by trying to cover it up. The best model builders admit their errors freely and learn from them quickly. Niels Bohr, the father of atomic physics, ascribed his success to making his mistakes faster than others. He also held that the opposite of any deep truth is also a deep truth, and routinely invited people to imagine the opposite of their pet theories and beliefs.

Bohr was a true dignitarian. So was Einstein. The two men disagreed profoundly on the nature of physical models, but the dialogue they conducted with each other on the subject is as exemplary for its respectfulness as it is famous for delineating a divide in the road of human thought.

People capable of handling social contradictions, artistic ambiguities, interpersonal disagreements, philosophical paradoxes, and identity crises—both their own and others'—are the opposite of ideologues. They cultivate equanimity and detachment and let go of self-righteousness and blaming. Should they forget, it is the nature of modeling to provide them with frequent lessons in humility. Mature model builders are problem solvers or artists in search of a synthesis that satisfies all parties.

Gandhi's truth-seeking strategy held that each person has a piece of the truth, but no one has the whole of it. The first step to a broader understanding is to take a strong stand for our piece, and then to engage in principled struggle with those who disagree. If we listen, more truth emerges from the process.[2] As Philo of Alexandria, the Hellenized Jewish philosopher who died in the year 50 CE, remarked: "Be kind, for everyone you meet is fighting a great battle."

Learning to see nature models as provisional has resulted in previously unimaginable technological and economic gains. A parallel transformation in which we open ourselves to changes in our social, political, and self models is our best hope for combating the rankism that now threatens to divide us hopelessly into a nation, and a world, of somebodies and nobodies.

Models have the extraordinary property of shielding individuals who espouse them from personal indignity. You can champion a model that turns out to be wrong, but that does not make you wrong. A model-building approach is inherently dignitarian, in stark contrast to the ideological posturing and put-downs that currently pervade politics and culture.

Moreover, models aim to reconcile all points of view, to account for everyone's perceptions, and to validate everyone's experience. In short, a good model is a synthesis (not a compromise) that makes everyone's perspective right in some respect.

There's no denying that we need beliefs, but we can get along quite nicely without absolutes. We cannot manage without working assumptions but we should resist elevating them into eternal verities. To know who we are does not mean we know who we'll become.

Moral codes are prescriptive behavioral models and, like all models, they evolve. This is not to say they are arbitrary or that "anything goes." That morals lack universality and infallibility does not mean we are free to ignore them where they do apply—just as the breakdown of Newtonian mechanics in the atomic realm does not render Newton's laws inapplicable to planets and projectiles. On the contrary, in certain domains, any particular moral principle will remain as valid as ever. Making such distinctions is part of learning to live in a post-fundamentalist world.

Identity in a Dignitarian Culture: A Self Model for the Twenty-First Century

Such are the facts in human experience . . . rich and poor, intelligent and ignorant, wise and foolish, virtuous and vicious, man and woman; it is ever the same, each soul must depend wholly on itself. . . . In the long, weary march, each one walks alone. . . .

This is a solitude which . . . every one of us has always carried with him, more inaccessible than the ice-cold mountains, more profound than the midnight sea—the solitude of self.

—Elizabeth Cady Stanton, American reformer
and women's suffrage leader

To address the relationships we have with institutions and with other individuals in an attempt to prune them of rankism, we need also explore a third, more primal relationship: the one we have with ourselves. All three of these relationships are constructs, or models, and as we've seen, the nature of models is to evolve.

But how can we talk of such change when it comes to our very identity? Like many, I chanced upon a tentative answer to this question in my teens, and like many, I didn't realize its full significance until I was considerably older. But over time, I came to see my identity for what it really is—a surprisingly fluid pastiche.

In high school science courses I noticed that everything we were being taught rested on assumptions. Yes, these assumptions were grounded in observation, but they were nonetheless assumptions, not unassailable truths. I accepted this absence of bedrock in science because the axiomatic approach seemed adequate to its goal, which was to describe how nature behaves. Moreover, on those rare occasions when the laws of science did fail us, there was always a remedy. We patched up the existing theory, or in the worst case scenario, abandoned it altogether and created a new and better one. No sentimentality. No clinging. No problem.

With regard to ordinary affairs, however, I was brought up to think that things were different. My parents and teachers all took it as self-evident that there were absolute verities when it came to people and their behavior. Science laws could change, albeit infrequently and only when confronted with irrefutable evidence. But unquestioning fidelity to a rigid set of timeless moral beliefs was taken as a measure of character.

But not long after my realization that scientific theories weren't carved in stone, the idea hit me that what was true in science was very likely also true in everyday life. One day, standing alone in my bedroom, it struck me that beliefs of every sort were fallible, and by the same token, subject to improvement. And that meant it was impossible to demonstrate beyond doubt that *anything* was absolutely true, once and for all.

It was as if, at that instant, I had suddenly grown up. The experience, although strangely liberating, was also sobering. My revelation left me feeling unmoored. And because my sense of self was shaken, I saw my identity as I might have seen someone else's—from the outside.

Before going downstairs to dinner that night, I decided to keep all this to myself, at least until I could defend it. I didn't want my parents to think I'd gone crazy. But a seed had been sown and for decades afterward, without understanding why, I was drawn to people and ideas that nurtured it.

My new perspective subtly affected the relationships I had with my friends. I began listening to them differently. Instead of judging what they did or said as right or wrong relative to some preordained standard, I drew them out and absorbed what they told me. Perhaps I was gathering information with which to put Humpty Dumpty together again. For whatever reasons, I became curiously nonjudgmental in responding to their troubles, and within a short time my circle of intimates began to expand.

After completing school and working for a dozen years—first as a physics professor and then as a college administrator—I took some time off to recover from burnout. It was toward the end of this phase that I recalled my high school epiphany. Then in my late thirties, I had accumulated enough personal history to see that over time I had indeed presented several rather different "selves" to the world. Like the evolving science models I had studied in school, I now saw that my identity, too, had undergone periodic metamorphoses. In addition to lots of incremental changes, I'd been a nobody, a somebody, and then a nobody again, with no end in sight to the cycle.

But if my persona could keep changing, then just who was I? And if this was also happening to others—and it seemed to me that it was— then who were they?

Self-understandings, like scientific theories, undergo continuing revision. I now see personal identity in model-building terms. Over time, we fabricate our sense of self bit by bit until, like a résumé, it gradually assumes individualized form and acquires a kind of totemic status. It feels "real" and permanent, but a close, moment-by-moment look reveals identity to consist of elements that are constantly in flux.

The "me" we ordinarily take ourselves to be is not an object in the classical sense, not a "thing" at all, but rather a provisional, working model. Despite our heroic efforts to pass as somebodies, we are all of us more tenuously assembled than we appear to be—none more so than newcomers to somebody status who mistake it for the be-all and end-all of life. Once this becomes clear, we realize it makes good sense for us to accord others the dignity we'd like for ourselves—at every stage in the journey, whatever our relative status.

To keep our identity in working order, we continually amend and burnish it, principally by telling and retelling our "story" to ourselves and anyone else who will listen. The older we get, the more we feel the need to rehearse and shore up the narrative, perhaps because we sense the possibility of our identity disintegrating into its constituent bits like the collapse of a rickety old shack.

Seeing personal identities as models allows us to see ourselves from a distance. It's easier to feel detached from a model than it is from a self-image. By understanding our identity as a particular model that we use at a given time under specific conditions, we gain the freedom to let go of pieces of it and allow new ones to replace them in response to changing circumstances. The feeling that life is a battle is replaced with the sense that it's a game played with opponents who, upon deeper reflection, are unmasked as allies.

Absent adversaries, it's almost impossible to raise our game to a higher level. With age, many come to this perspective. Former antagonists—colleagues, spouses, parents—are seen to have been essential participants in one's development. Accessing a dignitarian outlook earlier in life can spare us and others from the consequences of self-righteous posturing and from inciting continuing rounds of conflict in an attempt to even the score. This is something Nelson Mandela learned in prison and later exemplified as he led South Africans toward reconciliation.

It's a concept that has been put well by many writers and poets: "If you hate a person, you hate something in him that is part of yourself. What isn't part of ourselves doesn't disturb us," said novelist Hermann Hesse. "Then farewell, Horace; whom I hated so/Not for thy faults, but mine," wrote English poet Lord Byron.

My own identity, which had rested on institutional affiliations, had to realign itself with a freelance life after I left the relative security of the academic world. Although the dissolution of an identity can bring on a case of the blues, it loses some of its sting once you've built several different personas over time. Wrote Philip Massinger, a sixteenth-century English dramatist: "True dignity is never gained by place, and never lost when honors are withdrawn."

During the 1960s, as her children left home, I watched my mother undergo a profound and painful transformation of identity. Unfortunately, the fundamental change in women's self models that was sweeping through the world at that time had come a little too late for her. If she could have seen her transition as a natural metamorphosis rather than a loss of her "real self," it might have made things easier.

In the past, most individuals' self models were under less external pressure to change than they are today. Until recently, men and women tended to do the same kind of work their entire lives, keep the same partners, reside in the same place. But now with career, spouse, and geographical changes becoming commonplace, identities are becoming less permanent. They're more apt to dissolve and recrystalize numerous times during a single lifetime.

The point is not simply that any particular self model might be in need of revision. It is that the very notion that our self models are solid and invariant is false—as erroneous as was the presumed immutability of the nature models that enjoyed the church's seal of approval in the past.

To see the world as changing and not include our identities in the flux is naïve. Moreover, we cannot expect to remodel our personal and institutional relationships if we are wedded to unchanging models of ourselves.

The Self: A Home for Identities

Perhaps Shakespeare put it best:

> But man, proud man!
> Drest in a little brief authority,
> Most ignorant of what he's most assur'd,
> His glassy essence, like an angry ape,
> Plays such fantastic tricks before high heaven
> As make the angels weep.[3]

What the author points out here is that it is the opacity of our prideful egos that blinds us to our "essence," our see-through identity. Four hundred years ago, Shakespeare recognized that the human persona is really a cut-and-paste job that is porous, transparent, "glassy." What better description of a model—those ephemeral, provisional, but vital constructs that so enhance our vision?

If at some point in our life we can't conjure up a serviceable identity, an uncomfortable feeling comes over us. We feel we're ceasing to exist in the eyes of others and even our own. We're becoming invisible—a nobody.

This is ultimately why human beings need dignity, deserve dignity, and in the end, will see fit to grant it to one another. As Pascal noted, "Man is but a reed, the weakest in nature; but he is a thinking reed." Self-hood is tenuous, fluid, and unstable. Identity has to be handled care-fully, as a gardener tends his prize roses. "Attention must be paid," insists Willie Loman's wife in Arthur Miller's *Death of a Salesman*.[4] As play-wright David Mamet wrote in a tribute to Miller, "To find beauty in the sad, hope in the midst of loss, and dignity in failure is great poetic art."[5] To deny dignity to someone is to deprive the solitary, vulnerable self the sustenance it has need of to make its humble offering in the world and fulfill its existential duty.

Over the course of our lifetime, various identities form and collapse. Even though our current one may feel like "the real thing," every iden-tity eventually shows its age and begins casting about for a stage exit. In observing that "one man in his time plays many parts,"[6] Shakespeare, like many an Eastern sage, saw that to be human is to inhabit a series of roles while at the same time being a member of the audience—a part of, yet simultaneously a witness to, "the human comedy."[7]

As we look back at our life, the stream of our former identities resem-bles a succession of guests in a hotel. We are no one of these transients but rather the hotel's proprietor, affording each visitor a temporary haven. From our lofty eyrie, we recognize ourselves as a home for iden-tities. Each of these evanescent selves deserves to be received, well treated, and when the time comes, bid farewell with dignity.

Growing up, my friends and I expected to be the same person for life, just as our fathers and mothers had been. But by the time I was fifty I could look back and identify several distinct personas that had taken up residence within and used me as a mouthpiece to make one or another case in the world. So could most of my friends. Initially we were embarrassed by this state of affairs, feeling it to be a sign of incon-stancy and failure. Now I see metamorphosing from one identity to the next as a natural extension of the development from childhood to adolescence to early adulthood and beyond. The more flexible, forgiving attitude that results from a malleable self model turns out to be the perspective we need to maintain our dignity in adversity and accord it to others in theirs. If we can't treat our current self with respect, what chance have we of doing so with anyone else?

Survival Tips for Dignitarians

To be human is not to know one's self. The "I" that we confidently broadcast to the world is a fiction—a . . . container for the volatile unconscious elements that divide and confound us. In this sense, personal history and public history share the same dynamic principle: both are fables agreed upon.

—John Lahr, theater critic

We don't so much build our first persona as we recognize it emerging out of consciousness like the developing image in a Polaroid photograph. Usually during adolescence, without any conscious effort on our part, a crude but serviceable tripartite identity assembles itself. It consists of:

- ▶ A sense of our place in the universe (traditionally referred to as our relationship to God)
- ▶ The first inklings of how we might contribute to the world (our relationship to society)
- ▶ Sources of recognition (our relationships with family, teachers, and friends who are serving as midwives to our nascent identity)

The principal task of adolescence is to solidify as much as possible this first persona to the point that it enables us to make our way in the world.

It is only later, when this identity has dissolved and morphed into another, that we gain some distance from it and begin to see it as replaceable machinery rather than our one true self. With the view that we are model builders, and in the absence of rankist intimidation, comes the opportunity to assume a less anxious and more conscious role in the fabrication of our personas. The following sections discuss techniques that people have used for centuries to guide them in forging new identities, connecting the tools and process to dignitarian values.

Witnessing

There's a part of us that watches our doings and overhears our thoughts—a neutral observer that monitors our experiences as if from the outside, witnessing what the Danish philosopher Sören Kierkegaard aptly called the "stages on life's way." This faculty stands apart from the rush of worldly life and simply takes note of what happens. The elderly will tell you that although their bodies and minds have changed, this "witness" hasn't aged at all. Even in old age, it's the same youthful, candid observer that it was when they first became aware of it as a child. At ninety, my father told me he felt the "one" looking out at the world through the "two holes in the fence" was the same one that had done so when he was a boy of five.

As the literary critic Harold Bloom points out, Shakespeare drew attention to the witness by creating characters such as Hamlet and Falstaff who, in soliloquy, overhear themselves.[8] It is this inner process that enables us to take stock of where we are and then steer a different course if we're unsatisfied with what we find.

When the spectacle of life becomes intense, the witness often recedes into the background, but continues observing no matter how turbulent things become. This unobtrusive monitoring faculty is detached and nonjudgmental. The critical voice we sometimes hear in our head is not that of the witness. Blaming ourselves is rather the result of internalizing the rankist agenda of others who would put us down. In contrast, our witness is a "secret sharer" that does not condemn us no matter what we do or what others think of us. It plays an indispensable part in the creation and re-creation of our personas by chronicling with a disinterested eye everything that goes on in our home for identities.

The witness looks both inward and outward. There is no part of our-selves to which we feel closer. It's a model builder's closest ally. Some regard it as the soul.

Questing

Isidore I. Rabi, a Nobel laureate in physics, remarked: "Every other Jew-ish mother in Brooklyn would ask her child after school: 'So? Did you learn anything today?' But not my mother. 'Izzy,' she would say, 'did you ask a good question today?'"[9]

Learning to catch a good question on the fly, no matter how sopho-moric it may seem, is a model builder's lifeblood. Questions indicate the path to a new personal identity by suggesting ways in which we might contribute something of ourselves.

Most of our ancestors were fully occupied with just the feeding of their families. So long as we're struggling to fulfill our basic needs, we can't afford to pay attention to the questions within us. Suppressed, they lie dormant and are passed along from generation to generation. We make do with traditional doctrine and dogma until our survival is assured.

But once there is leisure, submerged questions surface into con-sciousness. They usually arise out of contradictions between ourselves and other people. The young unearth the questions their parents avoided and soon embark on their own search for answers.

The late writer Wallace Stegner said, "The guts of any significant fic-tion—or autobiography—is an anguished question."[10] Our inquiries generate our individuality. Even when we're unaware of them, they shape our every move.

As a teenager, Einstein wondered what time the clock in the steeple of his hometown Ulm, Germany, would show if the trolley he was on were to race away from it at the speed of light. It seemed to him that if the trolley left at noon and moved in sync with the light that showed the hands of the clock straight up, he would just keep on seeing noon for-ever. But wouldn't that mean that time had stopped? Thus was a ques-tion born, the pursuit of which would unlock some of the deepest mysteries of the universe.

In the places where we're most alive we are questions, not answers. One has to listen carefully, again and again, to detect new ones, which often make their presence known in a whisper.

Every person is an original, each of us unprecedented.[11] Even if our genes were cloned, our social environments would be distinct. This double uniqueness is further differentiated by the questions we generate, which are the source of our passions.

Taking our questions seriously, whether or not we are able to answer them, defines a personal quest that places our current identity on the line, exposing it to transformation. In a dignitarian society we would be able to do this without fear of humiliation or persecution.

In the film *My Name Is Nobody,* a young gunslinger who calls himself "Nobody" faces down a legendary old hand who has a reputation for being the "fastest gun in the West." In their climactic showdown, Nobody ostensibly kills Jack Beauregard, played by Henry Fonda. Written on his gravestone we see, "Nobody was faster than Jack Beauregard." While expressing the literal truth, this epitaph, via its twofold meaning, preserves the dignity of Beauregard, who, as it turns out, has actually faked his death and begun a new life on the Mississippi in partnership with the young man named Nobody.

In this same sense, nobody is holier than thou. Who is this nobody? It is the tiny interior voice that is trying to draw your attention to a new question, usually one that challenges a habitual behavior or belief. No one is holier than thou and no piece of us has a stronger claim to holiness than the unpretentious little nobody within. The universe rarely yells at us, but it's constantly whispering. If God has a voice, this is it.

Attempts to identify and express our unique selves are invariably fraught with self-doubt and suffering. Dislodging old beliefs and stale identities, thereby making way for new ones, is a crucial part of the process. This is often initiated by other peoples' criticisms and provocations. If those criticisms are proffered in a nonrankist manner we are more likely to be able to avoid a defensive response and instead internalize all sides of the matter at hand. Once that happens, synthesis, and with it a new self model, are usually within reach.

The Knights of the Round Table formed their identities in pursuit of the holy grail. Questing lives, as Carolyn Heilbrun argued in her classic *Writing a Woman's Life,* are now, at last, a real option for women as well as men.[12] Today's grail quests are apt to begin with a heartfelt question. Identifying our questions and pursuing them wherever they take us—while respecting this same process in others—is the modern counterpart of chivalric adventure, and it's no less heroic. The eternal search for human dignity finds no more evocative expression than the Arthurian quest for the holy grail.

Loving

According to Russian-born painter Marc Chagall, "In our life there is a single color, as on an artist's palette, which provides the meaning of life and art. It is the color of love."[13] And German philosopher Friedrich Nietzsche wrote: "Look back upon your life and ask: What up to now have you truly loved, what has raised up your soul, what ruled it and at the same time made it happy? Line up these objects of reverence before you, and perhaps by their sequence they will yield to you a basic law of your true self. Compare these objects and see how they form a ladder on which you have so far climbed up toward yourself."[14]

In addition to imitatively absorbing elements of our personal identity from beloved individuals, both living and dead, our persona is constructed from bits and pieces of cherished books, movies, music, and art. It is often through them that the first inklings of weakness in a model are revealed and alternative approaches suggested. For example, sensibilities that first take root in a poet, a novelist, an artist, or a dancer may become commonplace decades later as his or her body of work is assimilated into the culture. In this way, art is often instrumental in establishing a new cultural consensus. American novelist Henry James pointed out, "Art derives a considerable part of its beneficial exercise from flying in the face of presumptions."[15]

Love is the polestar guiding us to these elements of identity, whether they manifest in people or in their creations. When we heed the call of passion we enter pell-mell into a learning process that provides the raw materials out of which we fashion our unique personas. Einstein believed love was a better teacher than duty. Keats said, "I am certain of nothing but the holiness of the heart's affections."[16]

Acting on the basis of what or who we love always involves risk, but within that risk lies the opportunity for transformation. Often we are beckoned to change the outward forms of our lives, and this can frustrate the expectations of family, friends, or even ourselves. At certain transitional points, we may have several loves and move from predominant involvement with one to another.

If we follow the call of passion in our work, we often find ourselves alone. Personal passion can take us to places that others don't value because results in these areas have yet to be incorporated into the group consensus. In matters close to our hearts we observe closely and take immense pains over details, whether they are poetic, athletic, culinary, aesthetic, or logical. Consequently, we tend to know more than others about the nooks and crannies of our own unique realm of concern long before we can give it coherent expression, let alone persuade anyone else of its significance. A high tolerance for "failure" and rejection is perhaps the single most important attribute required for success. But as societies become more dignitarian, failure is not seized upon as a cause for rejection and we are not as hampered in our process by fear of stigma.

If economic necessity forces us to work for others, we may nonetheless remain faithful to our passion, purposefully making time to pursue it in one way or another. There is a feeling of homecoming when, after a day spent on other activities earning a living, our attention returns to our special area of interest.

The Dutch philosopher Spinoza ground eyeglasses while he composed his treatises. T. S. Eliot wrote poems while working in a bank. Einstein was employed in a patent office during the time when he was revolutionizing physics.

Countless men and women hold a day job while simultaneously pouring their creativity into an avocation or raising children. Often there is an option that can satisfy both our passion and our pocketbooks if we remain open to a solution that deviates from conventional pictures of success.

Sometimes work we seem to have been drawn into accidentally or by financial necessity turns out to be closer to our real concerns than were our fantasies, which are often shaped by beguiling stories of fame and fortune. The same problems turn up everywhere because they are unsolved everywhere. Hence, some version of the particular problem that defines our true task usually presents itself wherever we are. The outer forms of the problem may vary as we move from job to job, but when the issues within them bring a familiar excitement, it's a sign that we're getting close to the unresolved questions that generate our fervor and define our uniqueness.

No one can isolate for another exactly what he or she is concerned with. Advice-givers have passions of their own and may try to enlist others in their projects. Parents often push for pursuits that appear to offer security because they don't want their children falling back on parental support.

Under pressure from families, advisers, or peers—especially when it is rankist—students may affect an interest in the prestigious or the fashionable and lose touch with their real passion. Gently exposing posturing and pretension—while taking care not to insult their dignity—can free them to attend to their own innate questions. There is a famous quote attributed to the Hasidic rabbi Zusya, "In the world to come I shall not be asked: 'Why were you not Moses?' I shall be asked: 'Why were you not Zusya?'"[17]

Seeing our own identities not so much as finished edifices but rather as works in progress propelled by our loves and our questions enables us to see other peoples' identities in the same way. The result is that we don't pigeonhole them, and this tends to induce reciprocal openness. Interactions become less like pitched battles and more like improvisational dances.[18]

Letting go of the idea of an immutable self and moving beyond fixed beliefs may be a little disconcerting at first, but it soon begins to feel invigorating and empowering. Establishing personal and social change as the norm is the body and soul of dignitarian culture.

A Foreseeable Challenge

In conclusion, here is a quick look at a development that at first glance might seem to put human dignity in extreme peril. (Those with a distaste for speculation are invited to skip it.)

Futurists are warning that by midcentury we will likely be confronted with an unprecedented threat to what it means to be human—the advent of sophisticated thinking machines.[19] It's one thing to use calculators that outperform us; it will be quite another to face appliances manifesting suprahuman intelligence. Picture a cute little gadget perched on your desk that, by any measure, is smarter than you are. We'll probably program such machines not to be condescending, but the knowledge that robots have taken over many creative tasks will clearly require some getting used to.

A glimpse of how we're apt to react to such a development is provided by looking at how we have responded to prior status demotions. Copernicus's contention that the earth circled around the sun—removing us from center stage—caused an uproar that lasted for centuries. Darwin's theory of evolution, which made us all descendants of apes, was initially scorned and continues to be rejected by some. If life is discovered in various stages of development on other planets, the effect will be to further undermine human claims to a central, unique role in the universe.

Through our previous humblings, however, people took some comfort in their presumed higher intelligence. How will it affect our identity if we're pushed off *that* pedestal? Realizing that the functions of mind—the last bastion of our supposed superiority—can be replicated by machines is reminiscent of the medical discovery that the heart, long seen as the seat of the soul, was simply a pump made of muscle. We've rarely handled such blows to our pride with grace.

Possessed of truly Promethean powers, yet faced with man-made creations that outperform us at what we see as our special talents, the inhabitants of a dignitarian world will find virtue in humility. After a few final displays of vanity, we'll probably make our peace with accepting the help of thinking machines much as parents reluctantly but ultimately accept advice from their grown offspring.

Smart machines with computation speeds that exceed currently available ones by a millionfold might well serve as the astronauts of the future, exploring worlds where our biochemistry is a handicap and theirs is an asset. The introduction of thinking machines would also provide a perfect opportunity for conducting the dignity impact studies on new uses of power discussed in chapter 2. And if proposals pass muster, we can further enlist the help of our silicon partners in projecting increasingly complex scenarios as we move forward.

Over time, what is most distinctive and precious about human beings could be preserved and incorporated into the machines that, with aid from our clever progeny, we may someday design to supersede us. Dignity will be challenged, yes—but expunged? Not by smart machines so long as we befriend them and make them our allies. If dignity is defeated, it will likely succumb at human hands in the way it has been most trampled upon in the past—through war.

GLOBALIZING DIGNITY 10

IT IS EXCELLENT TO HAVE A GIANT'S STRENGTH;
BUT IT IS TYRANNOUS TO USE IT LIKE A GIANT.
—WILLIAM SHAKESPEARE, *MEASURE FOR MEASURE*

WAR'S A GAME, WHICH,
WERE THEIR SUBJECTS WISE,
KINGS WOULD NOT PLAY AT.
—WILLIAM COWPER

I KNOW NOT WITH WHAT WEAPONS WORLD WAR III WILL BE FOUGHT,
BUT WORLD WAR IV WILL BE FOUGHT WITH STICKS AND STONES.
—ALBERT EINSTEIN

The "Evolutionary Blues"

EVERYONE HAS KNOWN the blues: you lose your job or your health, your partner leaves you or your dog dies. Sorrow is an inescapable part of the human condition. You don't need the wisdom of the Buddha to know that life is suffering.

The evolutionary blues consist of sterner stuff, affecting not just an individual but our species as a whole.[1] These are the growing pains that accompany the political, cultural, environmental, and existential crises that have beset humankind throughout its bloody history. They stem from man's inhumanity to man and are carved deeply into the human soul. This book argues that building a dignitarian world can mitigate the evolutionary blues. By confronting rankism in its fiercest guises we have a chance to unsaddle at least some of the Four Horsemen of the Apocalypse and put their fearsome steeds to pasture.

We learn history as the history of wars. They stand out as terrible course corrections in our social evolution. As many are now warning, the advent and spread of weapons of mass destruction herald catastrophe for our species in this century if we don't find a peaceful way to complete the epochal transition from predation to cooperation.

Before suggesting a dignitarian alternative to war, I want to take a farewell look at it as it lives in our imagination. Only as we see through war's deceptive promise can we end our dependence on it and bid it adieu.

A World War in My Sandbox

Fighting Nazis and finding love—that's what my life is about.
      —Scott Simon, *Weekend Edition,* National Public Radio

For my friends and me, World War II was a game we played in the sandbox. The less popular kids had to be Nazis. Pearl Harbor was reenacted hundreds of times because it justified what followed—we fought back against our enemies and gradually turned the tide. Sandbox wars ended in massive bombing raids on "Berlin" and "Tokyo"—the Axis always lost because the Allies "controlled the skies."

In school there were air raid drills, but despite life-and-death exhortations from the principal, for us they were comical. No bombs ever fell. After all, didn't we control the skies? On Sunday evenings the family gathered around the radio—which stood on the floor and was a big as a bureau—to hear Walter Winchell's news bulletin "to all the ships at sea." I loved the hushed intensity in the room as we listened. Churchill's "blood, toil, tears, and sweat" speech still gives me chills.

The most powerful memories from those years are not events. Pearl Harbor, Hitler's death, and the dropping of the atomic bomb pale beside the patriotic feeling of everyone being united in a noble cause. Even kids had a part. Mine was to collect used tin cans and help my mother in our "victory garden," and I did so without complaint. The thought of dissenting from this war simply did not arise. In one voice, we vowed to force our enemies to "surrender unconditionally."

World War II ended with a bang. I was only nine but I remember just where I was standing when I heard about The Bomb. My father told me that it harnessed a new kind of energy, the energy of the sun. This scientific first interested me less than something unprecedented in his voice—awe, tinged with alarm. Throughout the war, he had always sounded confident that things were under control. Now his tone warned that things would never be the same. Not long afterward, newspapers proclaimed the advent of the "atomic age."

A Dignitarian Alternative to War

A century ago, the American psychologist William James famously called for a "moral equivalent to war," and people have been trying to come up with a better "game" ever since. So spellbound are we by war's glories and horrors, we fail to notice that it performs an important, if amoral, function. War can deliver an entire people to an open fluid place wherein they become capable of changing direction and embarking on a new course. For "losers" this can mean a fresh start, for "victors" an affirmation of their collective identity. This applies not only to the soldiers who do the fighting but also to those who stay behind and are thrust into new roles. For example, World War II transformed the lives of women, as was symbolized by Rosie the Riveter.

War and tribalism—or nationalism, its modern-day counterpart— have gone hand in hand precisely because the tribe—or nation—is the locus of our group identity and the battlefield is where it has historically been forged or shattered. The guilty knowledge that physical combat has been an instrument of identity transformation has surely been a barrier to finding a viable alternative to it. That is the reason for the deep ambivalence we feel toward war. We speak openly of our hatred for battle but hide our fascination with it. When we are not actually *at* war, it often lurks in our imaginations as an enticing adventure. To end our dependence on war as a means of affirming or changing identity, we need to find a dignitarian alternative for accomplishing the vital task of periodic social transformation.

Not long after James's call for a moral equivalent to war, H. G. Wells unknowingly answered it with a statement destined to become equally famous: "Human history becomes more and more a race between education and catastrophe."[2] To see war as a problem whose solution is education was prescient at the time. But education—at least the kind available during the twentieth century—did not keep us from going to battle.

What sort of learning might accomplish this critical goal? I believe that, paradoxically, it is the very skill that has, via technological development, made war so dangerous; the moral equivalent of war can be found in the conscious, dedicated pursuit of model building.

At first glance, this might seem too cerebral an activity to compete with the guts and glory of war. A closer examination, however, reveals that model building undercuts our dependence on war in three ways. William James couldn't realize this because in his time modeling was considered applicable only to nature, and the self was held to be something apart from nature.

For starters, model building develops and facilitates the capacity to change our minds, to replace one belief system with another, to transform our understanding of the world, and to evolve new personal and group identities. While we have relied on violence to achieve these tasks in the past, contemporary model-building skills afford us an alternative that is at once less destructive and more precise. Modeling goes to the very crux of identity formation and reformation, and it does so without destruction of property or loss of life.

Once we give up the notion that we *are* our personas, we can let *them* do battle in our stead rather than putting our lives on the line. Our ideas and beliefs can be sent into "combat" and defended to *their* death, not ours. The ultimate deterrent to war is not the threat of retaliation, but the availability to both sides of more cost-effective methods of self and group transformation. (The situation that arises when one party to a conflict absolutely insists on settling it with brute force is the subject of the next section, "What About Bad Guys?")

Second, there is the richness, excitement, and fulfillment that we experience in exercising our model-building skills. It's not hard to imagine the exhilaration that must have accompanied modeling and then constructing the first airplane, nuclear reactor, or computer. Less obvious is the fact that the satisfactions of model building do not depend on resultant fame. What brings genuine satisfaction is the ongoing pursuit of our own interests, contributing the fruits of our labors, and acknowledgment of those contributions.

People involved in model building, no matter what the field, are less susceptible to the drumbeat of war because they are already fully engaged. They are immune to demagogic calls to battle because their personal quests feel as heroic and noble to them as any military undertaking. In the past, when many were stuck in routine lives devoid of excitement, going to war could seem like an adventure. But as model building, in all its captivating varieties, is practiced in ever increasing numbers, it will act as a vaccine that confers partial immunity to martial seductions.

Finally, model building can be applied to the very political contradictions that in the past have triggered violent conflict. A team of model builders—people who have traditionally been called diplomats, mediators, or negotiators—can be assigned the task of coming up with a metamodel that embraces and resolves the competing positions of potential adversaries. Such comprehensive models allow for change—not only of one's own mind and of the opponent's, but also of the world—without resort to war.[3]

Faith in the belief that a unifying model can be found is analogous to faith in the existence of one God. Monotheism is the theological counterpart of the model builder's belief in the ultimate reconcilability of apparently contradictory observations, or positions, into a single, self-consistent framework. In this setting, the proverb "God is love" testifies to the belief that there exists a unitary framework in which apparently contradictory, antagonistic pieces of the whole can nonetheless be brought into harmony. Model building, like love, is inclusive and unifying. This goes to the heart of why it is such a valuable tool in building a dignitarian world. Not only can we use it to anticipate indignities, but the end product—a synthesizing model—reveals everyone's contribution to the whole. Wrote English novelist John Fowles:

> "I'm still defeated by the conundrum of God.
>   But I have the devil clear."
> "And what's he?"
> "Not seeing whole."[4]

With the advent of a dignitarian world, humankind will set war aside like children putting away their toy soldiers for the last time. We will honor all those who fought for us as we now honor pioneers and explorers. They were pushing into the unknown on our behalf, in the only way we knew how at the time. But now we have a better way—one that will spare the men and women at the front from having to make the ultimate personal sacrifice in our collective quest for truth.

People give up power only to grasp greater power. They abandon a familiar game only to take up a better one. Model building is a better game than war.[5] Compared to the dialogues of model builders, the slogans of demagogues sound like the braggadocio of adolescents. Compared to model building, war is not only clumsy; it is boring.

What About Bad Guys?

Over the last century, wars do appear to have been declining, both in frequency and intensity.[6] But even if aggression is becoming less likely with the passage of time, it can never be completely ruled out. Any group can choose to destroy the peace and may well do so if it thinks it can get away with it. This means we must always be prepared to face such an opponent—whether it be an individual committing a crime, a group engaging in terrorism or genocide, or a nation declaring war—in a more elementary struggle wherein brute force determines the outcome.

The durability of any post-rankist framework is bought at the price of preparedness to meet "bad guys"—those who refuse to play by the new rules—on their own turf. To make and keep the brute force option unappealing, a credible superior force, willing and able to disqualify or dominate aggressors, must be kept in readiness and in sight. Just as referees and umpires prevent cheating and police deter crime, so a strong defense—national and/or supranational—is required to deter rogue organizations or states.

From the perspective of human social evolution, we can see ourselves as now emerging from a long history of predation, as suggested by statistics on war-related deaths given in footnote 6 of this chapter. As we make this transition, it's all-important that we erect steep barriers to slipping back into our old ways. By doing so we should in time be able to make transgressive criminal lapses rare. The most important thing we can do to avoid having to resort to force, however, is to make sure that everyone has an opportunity to contribute to the whole.

Malrecognition and Counterterrorism

Trying to identify a single "root cause" of terrorism is a futile endeavor. Indeed, it is clear that the psychological, political, cultural, and religious motivations of the individuals who actually plan and execute acts of terror are complex and varied.[7] As the Russian novelist Dostoevsky put it: "While nothing is easier than to denounce the evildoer, nothing is more difficult than to understand him." Fortunately, we do not need to understand the precise motivations of terrorists to mount a defense against their activities.

Why? Because the reasons that bystanders sympathize with terrorists and ennoble them as "martyrs" are not so difficult to understand, and by addressing those reasons we can marginalize the activists. Sympathizers generally see the activists as protesting chronic indignities with which they, too, identify. Regardless of the individual psychology of the activists, a developing wisdom suggests that terrorism, as a strategy, is adopted in reaction to what is perceived by a larger group of sympathizers as organized dominance behavior that is to their detriment. Although bystanders generally limit their own protests to passive resistance and noncooperation, they are not displeased when those they see as their oppressors are made to suffer at the hands of their activist compatriots.

In the aftermath of an act of terrorism it is often possible to catch a glimpse of the extent of the latent support for activist perpetrators. Following the attacks of 9/11, thousands of disenfranchised young Muslims, many with little concern for the precise political aims of the Al Qaeda leadership, celebrated in the streets of foreign capitals. This often happens in instances of domestic terrorism as well. In the weeks following the shootings at Columbine High School, throngs of school outcasts all over the United States voiced complaints about intolerance, humiliation, and bullying. Similarly, when an employee goes "postal," browbeaten workers from near and far, while distancing themselves from the violence, begin urging their employers to appoint ombudspersons.

The extent to which active terrorists depend on passive sympathizers for material and psychological support varies from one situation to the next. But for there to be a renewable supply of purveyors of violence and suicide bombers, volunteers for such missions need to feel they are making a statement on behalf of a group whose members regard them as heroic martyrs. They want to believe that their sacrifice will not only bring recognition to themselves personally but will also draw attention to indignities suffered by the entire class of people with whom they identify.

Any cause that can draw significant numbers of passive adherents out of their latency poses a grave threat to the status quo. The Gandhi-led struggle for Indian independence, the American civil rights movement, and the people-power revolutions in Soviet satellites (including Poland, Hungary, and East Germany) and former republics (the Baltic nations, Georgia, Ukraine) showed the world what happens when those suffering in silence find a way to act out their resentment.

For centuries, African Americans stoically resigned themselves to slavery and, after their emancipation, to menial jobs in a segregated, racist society. Protest had to remain covert because open rebellion was summarily punished. In the 1960s, under the leadership of Dr. Martin Luther King, Jr., the Gandhian strategy of nonviolent civil disobedience gave millions of people who were passive sympathizers an acceptable way to cross over into activism. Huge numbers of them marched in the streets and subjected themselves to arrest and police brutality while the world watched with mounting apprehension.

As the ranks of nonviolent protestors swelled, Congress had no recourse but to begin dismantling deeply entrenched segregationist barriers to equal opportunity, and initiated a series of reforms to eliminate degrading societal practices. Faced with escalating disruption, Americans realized that evil lay not in the protestors but in the racism that fueled their outrage.

To combat terrorism, societies must of course pursue and neutralize violent extremists just as they do criminals within their borders and aggressor nations. Governments will have to learn to counter the open-source, guerilla strategies employed by terrorist networks with innovative methodologies of their own.[8] But no matter how sophisticated the counterterrorist strategy, the ultimate outcome of the struggle hinges on preventing a wholesale shift of passive supporters to active terrorism. As *New York Times* columnist Thomas Friedman writes, "The greatest restraint on human behavior is what a culture and a religion deem shameful."[9] We're unlikely to succeed in eradicating terrorism unless we alleviate the systemic indignities that depreciate lives and lead onlookers to ally themselves with extremists. However, once that sympathy is gone—and with it, all manner of psychological and material support—the chances of shutting down terrorism improve greatly.

We inhabit a world in which millions of individuals, informed by radio and television, can see that their potential to contribute to the world is being thwarted—by whom matters less than that regrettable reality. There is nothing more combustible than hordes of bored young people suffering from chronic malrecognition. Embittered and with nothing left to lose, they are shopping for an identity in which they can take pride. Unless they can lead better lives—lives of engagement and recognition—they remain ready recruits for violence, even if only as supporting players helping to carry out the agenda of a leadership whose incentives and motives may well be different from their own.

Terrorists can also be drawn from the ranks of a relatively privileged but alienated and angry middle class if they can be persuaded they would be acting on behalf of a greater good. The London suicide bombers of July 2005, like the March 2004 bombers in Madrid, joined the global jihad after radicalization by extremist Islamic teachings. The willingness to kill innocents is dependent in part on the belief that one is connected to a cause larger than oneself.

Terrorism itself is an extreme manifestation of rankism. Eliminating it will require removing sources of chronic, ill-considered provocation. The reforms spurred by the civil rights and women's movements opened doors to education and jobs that had previously been closed to blacks and women. Opportunity worked before, and it will work again. Opportunity is really all that ever works because without it there can be no dignity. But now it must be provided the world over. Facilitating this internationally and conforming the foreign policies of developed countries to such a goal will be difficult, but not impossible. Among other things, it requires systematically identifying and eliminating rankism in relations with other societies, cultures, and nations.

In a world where the weak can threaten a superpower—a world in which experts warn that an act of nuclear terrorism is likely—it is a vital part of self-defense to ensure that national policies are manifestly respectful, fair, and just. Wherever there is domination, paternalism, condescension, exploitation, occupation, or colonization—in short, wherever there is humiliation and indignity—there will be indignation, and a few of the angry will volunteer for what they and their admirers see as martyrdom. Passive aggression and violent outbursts in the workplace and schools, computer sabotage, terrorism, genocide, and war all have their origins in chronic malrecognition.[10]

Seeing terrorism in such a light does not excuse it any more than attributing a theft to poverty does. Nor can it prevent some individuals from committing isolated acts of terrorism for reasons of their own. But without taking into account the effects of systemic malrecognition on maintaining a supportive base for terrorism, any counterterrorism strategy is incomplete and doomed to fail. It's like addressing dysentery with high-tech antibiotics while ignoring the fact that the water supply is contaminated.

Eliminating malrecognition is a generational task, like going to Mars or ending world hunger, and in some ways is even more complex. Whereas malnutrition cripples individuals and occasionally rises to the level of famine, it is not contagious. In contrast, malrecognition spreads because when our dignity is offended, our first impulse is to reciprocate in kind. The twentieth century demonstrated that war, unlike famine, can leap easily and quickly from one continent to another. So can terrorism. Indeed, it already has.

By pursuing nonrankist international policies that safeguard the dignity of all, we can support a nonviolent democratic approach to the inescapable challenge of the twenty-first century: achieving global social justice.

Handling "Domestic Violence" in the Global Village

Just decades ago, the proverb "A man's home is his castle" was interpreted to mean that what the head of the family did within his home to his wife and children was none of the public's business. If someone took it upon himself to intervene, that person was regarded as a meddler or vigilante. Now there are laws—and the willingness to enforce them—that apply to family matters. When it comes to domestic abuse, the burden of proof has shifted from the presumed victims to the alleged victimizers. One phone call is all it takes to have the police knocking on, or knocking down, the door to the home of a spouse or parent suspected of violence.

As the world becomes a global village, it is natural that what have been regarded as sovereign national domains become subject to the watchful eyes, and under dire circumstances, the forceful intervention, of neighboring states. A famine in Ethiopia or Somalia; a genocide in Cambodia, Uganda, Rwanda, Bosnia, or the Sudan; an earthquake in Iran, Turkey, or Pakistan; a tsunami in Southeast Asia; the HIV-AIDS pandemic; a hurricane like Katrina—all are rapidly becoming everybody's problem and everybody's business.

At what point does our responsibility to fellow human beings warrant the abrogation of a nation's sovereignty? In the late twentieth century, we grappled with this question as it applied to our neighbors down the street and decided that the rights of battered spouses and abused children outweighed those of the "man in his castle." In the twenty-first century we have to answer the same question as it applies to the neighbors with whom we share this ever-shrinking planet.

An important step toward a dignitarian world is to fashion rules that tell us under what circumstances to override state sovereignty and intervene. And we need to create the global analogue of standing municipal Emergency Response Teams—variously referred to as Rapid Response Forces or SWAT teams—to enforce the rules governing intervention.[11]

In the case of natural disasters such as earthquakes and floods, the victims and their governments usually invite outside assistance. But for man-made horrors such as torture, murder, and genocide associated with despots and police states, there is not only the resistance of the perpetrator but typically disagreement among outsiders about the proper course of action.

Former President Clinton now regards not stepping in during the Rwandan genocide as the biggest mistake of his presidency, and he has formally apologized. In the final weeks of his term of office, President George H. W. Bush did order the military to enter Somalia and a genocidal famine was halted. Estimates are that this saved the lives of hundreds of thousands, notwithstanding the view of many Americans that the mission was a failure due to the subsequent loss of life and horrific broadcast images that followed the shooting down of a Black Hawk helicopter. If powerful nations have the ability to stop a genocide, it is hard to make the case that the right thing to do in dire situations is nothing.

But just as with the police who knock down the door to a man's home to stop him from beating his wife, when sovereignty is breached and intervention undertaken, it has to be done correctly. Great care must be exercised to minimize the harm done to innocents. The FBI raid on the Branch Davidian compound at Waco, Texas, in April 1993, in which seventy-six cult members died, is an example of a failed intervention, one that linked SWAT teams with the use of unnecessary force and tarnished their reputation across the country. But in truth, despite some notable excesses, the majority of these teams consist of highly trained professionals who represent society's frontline response to volatile situations and who exercise great skill in delicate and dangerous circumstances.

Obviously, it is not always wise or even possible to become involved, especially in the internal affairs of a state. The price may be too high, the risk of doing damage too great. Every case must be decided in light of the particulars. As with domestic abuse, there is no single formula for right action, but it's better to do nothing than to make a bad situation worse. Sadly, the latter has often been the case in international interventions, in part because some states have used the alleged misbehavior of others as a pretext to advance their own agendas.

But in recent decades there has been increased willingness, for reasons unique to each circumstance, to confront abusive regimes in other countries. The Vietnamese intervened to stop the Khmer Rouge's genocide in Cambodia in 1979; the Tanzanians did so to put an end to Idi Amin's despotism in Uganda; and more recently, NATO stepped in to halt ethnic cleansing in Bosnia and Kosovo.

In 2005 the United Nations acknowledged limits to state sovereignty by adopting the principle that states have a responsibility to protect their citizens from war crimes, crimes against humanity, and genocide. More to the point, the U.N. recognized that if a state fails to do this, the international community has an obligation to act. In other words, the U.N.'s so-called responsibility-to-protect principle creates a legal and moral framework for intervening in the next Rwanda, Somalia, Kosovo, or Darfur. The U.N. Security Council now has an explicit mandate to act as the world's policeman, but unlike the standing police forces of cities, these international "cops" are hired and deployed on a case-by-case basis and only as the Council sees fit.

One thing is becoming obvious. To be effective, military intervention usually needs to be multilateral and also part of a larger package that includes humanitarian assistance, economic development, and subsequent rebuilding of social and civic institutions. The analogy with domestic abuse holds. After an intervention, social workers try to ensure that net harm does not befall the family as a result of removing the offending party.

Creating a ready multinational capability to intervene in a timely fashion in the sovereign affairs of nations guilty of abusing their own citizens remains one of the great unfinished tasks bequeathed by the twentieth century to the twenty-first. It will take dignitarian states to field global emergency response teams in a fair and proper manner, but doing so is an essential part of owning the power that is ours.

RELIGION IN A DIGNITARIAN WORLD 11

> IF THERE IS NO GOD,
> NOT EVERYTHING IS PERMITTED TO MAN.
> HE IS STILL HIS BROTHER'S KEEPER
> AND HE IS NOT PERMITTED TO SADDEN
> HIS BROTHER,
> BY SAYING THAT THERE IS NO GOD.
> —CZESLAW MILOSZ, POLISH NOBEL LAUREATE IN LITERATURE

> THIS CENTURY WILL BE DEFINED BY A DEBATE THAT
> WILL RUN THROUGH THE REMAINDER OF ITS DECADES:
> RELIGION VERSUS SCIENCE. RELIGION WILL LOSE.
> —JOHN MCLAUGHLIN, AMERICAN TALK SHOW HOST

> THE EYE WITH WHICH I SEE GOD IS
> THE SAME EYE WITH WHICH GOD SEES ME.
> —MEISTER ECKHART, THIRTEENTH-CENTURY GERMAN MYSTIC

RELIGION IS AT ONCE humanity's consolation and its divider. As individuals, we turn to religion for solace. The concept of the soul invests our existence with a kind of transcendence and helps us cope with the harsh reality that, as Thomas Hobbes famously wrote, life is often "nasty, brutish, and short." The idea of God not only serves as a repository for all we do not yet understand—and there will always be plenty of that—but also provides us with a certain dignity. For that reason alone, religion cannot be omitted in discussing a dignitarian world.

Religion: Dignifier of Humankind

Religions the world over teach the sanctity of human dignity. Theistic religions go further and proclaim the existence of a personal, caring God. Given the supreme importance of dignity and our own spotty record when it comes to according it to each other, it's the rare person who, when all worldly options seemed exhausted, has not wished for divine intervention. In extremis, even skeptics are apt to question, if not suspend, their disbelief. Under dire circumstances, they, too, are prone to hope, if not pray, for some sort of suprahuman or supernatural source of respect. As the "dignifier of last resort," God comforts us through all the stages on life's way.

But despite, or perhaps because of, its place of privilege in the human heart, religion has also been the root of much conflict. It has divided individuals, groups, and entire cultures one from another, and has been invoked as a rationale for violence and war.

These diametrically opposed uses of religion—to confirm the dignity of those who share the faith while sanctioning indignity toward people of a different faith or no faith at all—have led to a polarization of attitudes regarding its role in society. Its potential to trigger debate and sow discord—not only between religion and science but more significantly among the various religions—has a long history that continues into the present. Some observers are even warning that religious conflict may escalate into a "clash of civilizations."[1]

It is impossible to picture a dignitarian world in which these divisive struggles are not resolved. The model-building perspective illuminates the complementarities of the conservative and progressive positions in politics. On the international front, it suggests a better game than war. How might it help assuage the contentiousness that has for so long been associated with religion?

Religion and Science

In previous chapters I've used quotations as pithy summaries of complex ideas. The McLaughlin epigraph at the head of this chapter serves a different purpose. Like much punditry, it's a provocation. Sorting out what's right and what's wrong about the prediction of this onetime Jesuit priest will help us identify the vital role that religion has to play in a dignitarian society.

When religion embraces a particular nature model, it usually does so fixedly. As a consequence, when science moves on to a new model, as it invariably does, religion is left advocating outdated beliefs. That's the position in which the Catholic Church found itself in 1600 in defending Ptolemy's earth-centered model of the solar system against the sun-centered Copernican one. It's the situation in which supporters of creationism—and its offspring, intelligent design—find themselves today.

Religion is not likely to win an argument with contemporary science by championing an earlier science model. Many religious leaders know this and cheerfully cede the business of modeling nature to scientists. Neither they nor the scientists who study these matters, many of whom are themselves people of faith, see any contradiction between the perennial wisdom embodied in the world's religions and, say, Darwin's theory of evolution, the geological theory of plate tectonics, or the Big Bang theory of the cosmos. For example, Tenzin Gyatso, the Dalai Lama, wrote in an op-ed piece in the *New York Times,* "If science proves some belief of Buddhism wrong, then Buddhism will have to change."[2]

That any of the scientific theories mentioned just above could, in principle, be incorrect or incomplete is taken for granted by the scientific world even though, as of today, there is no evidence that contradicts them unambiguously. Darwin's theory of evolution, Newton's laws of motion, and quantum theory are, of course, "just theories." But each of them is an extremely useful and accurate one. Applied within their domains of validity, they all work well. No society can fully avail itself of modern technology without the guidance provided by these models.

As long as religion doesn't take positions on nature models, it can avoid ending up stranded with a set of obsolete convictions, and find itself defending an old nature model against a new, improved one. If that's what McLaughlin meant, he's right, but he isn't telling us anything Galileo didn't know.

Religion and Values

Just as religion finds itself challenging science when it identifies with particular nature models, so, too, when it enters the realm of values and politics, must it expect to compete for hearts and minds with evolving social and political models. Here the case is not as clear-cut as with nature models because it is typically much harder to demonstrate the superiority of a new social or political model than it is of a new nature model. The evidence is often ambiguous, even contradictory, partly because intangible personal preferences play a much larger role. As everyone who has argued politics is aware, the "facts" cited by partisans in support of their policy choices are often as debatable as the policies themselves.

Like nature models, political and social models are shaped by human experience, and as experience accumulates, models by necessity change. Religious models could, in principle, keep pace, but generally they tend to lag behind the emerging social consensus. Why? Because the morals espoused by religion have usually proven their worth over very long periods of time. Hence, the first impulse is to insist that behaviors that contradict these ethical models be forced into conformity with them. This conservative stance not only avoids risk but also affirms the power of the presiding authorities, just as the church's opposition to the Copernican model did.

The fact that tradition is often, but not infallibly, right goes to the essence of the eternal wrangling that has long divided empirical and ecclesiastical teachings. Resolving this schism will close an open wound that must be healed in order to firmly ground a dignitarian society.

What is now traditional was not always so. To see inherited values as absolute truths handed down from on high fails to recognize that they earned their stripes in competition with alternative precepts that lost out. It's important to acknowledge that millions of lives were sacrificed to establish the values we now live by. The bloodiest wars, however horrible, often played a part in forging our human identity and its many cultural variations.

In this view the term "moral" does not gain its legitimacy as "received wisdom" set forth in holy writ or passed down from divine to human hands. Rather, it is a prescriptive model based on close observation, intuition, and extrapolation. Prophets like Moses, Buddha, Lao-tzu, Mo-tzu, Jesus, Muhammad, Sankara, and others are seen as extraordinarily perceptive philosophers with an uncanny knack for the long view (in particular, for discerning behaviors that foster long-term social equilibrium).[3] Then and now, moral precepts can be understood to be grounded in an empirical knowledge of cause and effect.

Take, for example, the commandment, "Thou shalt not kill." It is not hard to imagine that witnesses to tit-for-tat cycles of revenge murders concluded that "not killing" was the way to avoid deadly multigenerational feuds and that someone—in this case, Moses—enshrined this realization for others and posterity. From a model-building perspective, it's plausible that all the Ten Commandments were assembled from the combined wisdom of a number of people. Drawing on the oral and written history of past and present generations and bearing close witness to their own psychodynamics, they realized that certain individual behaviors ran counter to personal stability or group solidarity, leaving oneself or one's community vulnerable to exploitation and domination. They labeled these practices "immoral," anticipating that over time economic, psychological, social, and political forces would bring about either their elimination or the decline and disappearance of individuals or groups who countenanced them.

These nuggets of moral genius, and many others of comparable significance, are recorded in the world's holy books. Distilled and refined through the ages, they constitute the ethical foundation of society. If somehow they were to disappear and we had to start over, we would, by trial and error and with much bloodshed, gradually rediscover them from scratch (think of William Golding's novel *Lord of the Flies*[4]). They are neither arbitrary nor is it mandatory to attribute them to revelation, though one is perfectly free to do so if one wishes. But we may equally suspect they were unearthed in the same way we discover everything else—through an arduous process of inquiry and testing. Having demonstrated their worth, they were then elevated to special status in a process similar to that which results in the formulation and promulgation of scientific models.

Understanding morality as evidence-based amounts to tracing general behavioral guidelines back to a complex set of empirical observations. Once we have done so, a given moral precept can stand as shorthand for the whole body of observations and reasoning that lies underneath. The ethical formulations of religion represent an accumulation of such proverbial phrases, which function as reminders and guides.

As with all models, these are not infallible. Further scrutiny can lead to their modification. More often, however, additional experience validates them. Exceptions have long been allowed to "Thou shalt not kill"—for example, capital punishment and warfare. But Moses may yet have the last word. As we move into the twenty-first century, the global trend to abolish capital punishment is unmistakable and the pressure to eliminate war is mounting. It's not even out of the question that someday—as we develop alternative sources of protein—we'll decide that this ancient commandment applies not only to our fellow human beings but to the animal kingdom as well.

Religion is the chief repository of the time-tested wisdom of the ages, the preeminent teacher of precepts that have acquired the mantle of tradition. But as every reformer knows, tradition has its downside. Old moral codes can stifle progress by strangling in the crib inklings of a better world. While the heavy hand of custom saves us from our worst, it too often seems to keep us from our best.

Together, tradition and precedent, sometimes fortified with assertions of infallibility, constitute a high hurdle that any new social or political model must clear. A case in point was the twentieth-century shift in the prevailing societal consensus on issues like race, gender, marriage, divorce, and sex. Only after decades of debate and strife did new values displace older ones. Where religious doctrine failed to adjust, the public gradually stopped paying it much attention. This has likely been a factor in the precipitous decline, since World War II, of church attendance in much of Europe. Over the long term, people increasingly looked not to their church, synagogue, or mosque for their views on how to live and how to vote, but rather to culture and politics.

As the distillation of centuries of learning, religion has much to offer the modern world. But when it attaches itself rigidly to certain social or political models it eventually loses relevance in those domains because models of any stripe that are not allowed to evolve are invariably abandoned.

To summarize, McLaughlin's prediction that religion will lose out to science by century's end is right in the trivial sense—already recognized by many religious leaders—that science typically espouses newer, better nature models than does religion. Similarly, when religion allies itself with a partisan political doctrine—no matter if it's left or right—it weds itself to the values of a particular time. That is what churchmen who supported Nazism did when they invoked their religious beliefs to further the state's nationalistic and anti-Semitic agenda. It is what religious supporters of segregation did in the American South. And it is what defenders of genital cutting are doing today. Political models and cultural values are evolving rapidly, and whenever religion aligns itself with partisan social models it can't expect to retain its hold over the young, on whom the weight of tradition falls far more lightly. To chain theology to the ship of state is to go down with it when it sinks.

What does this perspective suggest regarding the current debate about same-sex marriage? In the end, the matter will be decided not by the victory of one or another interpretation of scripture, but by reference to emerging social values, very much in the way the disagreements over slavery, and a century later, over segregation, were decided. As it became clear that second-class citizenship was indefensible, attempts to justify these practices through religion were abandoned, and instead, religious values were enlisted on behalf of emancipation and desegregation.

On the other hand, if either science or politics believes it will succeed in marginalizing religion, it is mistaken. Religion is vulnerable when it encroaches on others' turf, but not when it sticks to its home ground, which is the self and its transformation.

Religion and the Self

It would be a mistake to conclude that a drop in church attendance means that interest in spiritual matters is diminishing. Despite the public's lack of fidelity to various nature and social models embraced by religion, it still holds a very special place in a great many hearts. Why is this?

When it comes to knowing the self and mapping its transformations, nothing holds a candle to religious models. The only competitors in the Western canon are to be found in literary classics such as those by Dante, Cervantes, Shakespeare, Milton, Melville, and Dostoevsky, whose works serve as handmaidens to the world's holy books.[5]

Examples of religious insight into the nature of the self and of the creative model-building process can be found in all the religious traditions. I'll cite just two here, drawn from Christianity and Hinduism, respectively—the doctrines of "resurrection" and "reincarnation." As applied to the physical body, these tenets are arguable. Nonbelievers reject them outright and even some believers take them metaphorically, not literally.

But as applied to the model-building process, they are profound and powerful. Models must "die to be reborn," none more dramatically than our self models. We who live by them, identify with them, and sometimes cannot separate our persona from a particular, familiar one, may well experience the disintegration of a self model as a kind of death. The struggle to come to terms with the loss of a partner or child, or with a sudden change in our status or health, can feel like what St. John of the Cross described as a "dark night of the soul."

From the model-building perspective, resurrection and reincarnation are evocative descriptions of the metamorphoses of identity that most of us experience over the course of a lifetime. Yes, the process occurs *within* one's lifetime rather than connecting one life span to another. But where can we find more luminous and consoling guidance for making life's most hazardous journeys than in the Bible, Talmud, Koran, Upanishads, and Sutras? That the core teachings in these books provide the most accurate guide to inner transformation is the reason they are deemed holy.

During those perilous passages wherein one self dissolves and another crystallizes in its place, we are at maximum vulnerability, like a crab molting its shell. When an old self begins to disappear, our defenses are down, and our dignity at high risk. At times the community we normally depend on to shore up our self-respect, even the fellowship of friends and family, can fail us, and we may find ourselves utterly alone.

When others deny our dignity, religion upholds it. For many, the idea of a personal god assures them that even in the darkest of times, when they may feel bereft of human support, they are valued, respected, and loved. This accounts for the relatively greater commitment to religion among peoples whose survival is precarious as well as for the common phenomenon of conversion during a life crisis.

Granted, individual priests, rabbis, roshis, and mullahs have sometimes failed to respect the dignity of those to whom they minister, adherents to other faiths, or of nonbelievers. But in their essential teachings, every religion testifies to the inviolable, sacred dignity of humankind, at all times and under all circumstances.

Religion is the tool of tools when it comes to becoming a new somebody. It combines art, literature, and theater in the context of communal fellowship to effectively transmit truths about the self and its transformation that are vital to maintaining our balance and creativity. No other body of knowledge offers more relevant and resonant teachings on what is one of humanity's most precious faculties—the intimate, intricate process of building models of ourselves. For this reason, the role of religion in a dignitarian culture is secure.

The Eye of God

Through an open skylight over my bed, I can see the phases of the moon, the stars, an occasional plane, and at dawn, soaring birds. A few sparrows have flown inside and soon found their way out again. Now and then a squirrel peeks over the edge. But apart from these locals, I do not feel seen as I spy on the cosmos.

On cold winter nights I sometimes imagine that I've drifted out the aperture and am floating in the near-absolute zero temperatures of empty space. In that subarctic infinitude, the earth is an igloo and we are all Eskimos. If other beings exist, we seem beyond their reach and they beyond ours. In any case, my thoughts go not to aliens but to the stars and the lifeless emptiness holding them.

Peering into its infinitude, I have no sense that the universe returns my gaze. Its eye is cold, if not blind. See someone seeing you and you exist. Look long enough into a fathomless void and you begin to ask, "Who am I? What am I doing here? Does anyone out there care?" My lifetime an instant, my body a speck, myself unremarked. The universe seems uncaring, the cosmic indifference of infinite space a blow to my dignity.

But then the old saying that "God helps those who help themselves" pops into my head. And President Kennedy's variant thereof: "Here on Earth, God's work must truly be our own." If instead of gazing outward, we turn our attention inward, we discover that the universe does indeed have a heart—in fact, it has lots of them. They are beating in our breasts.

Any inventory of the cosmos that omits human beings is like a survey of the body that overlooks the brain. In evolving the human mind, the universe has fashioned an instrument of self-understanding and empathy. We are that instrument, and since we are part of the cosmos, we err if we judge it to lack kindness, love, and compassion. If we believe the universe is heartless, it's because we do not love.

But what if the impersonal forces that extinguished the dinosaurs should hurl a comet at us? There's a crucial difference between that time and now. The demise of the dinosaurs made room for the appearance of mammals and thus for Homo sapiens. In the sixty-five million years since the dinosaurs vanished, there evolved a creature possessed of sophisticated model-building skills. If we use our talents wisely, they will enable us to avoid all manner of potential catastrophes—those of our own making as well as hurtling asteroids with our names on them.

The passage to a dignitarian world will take time, and it will not always be smooth. We have yet to lift a billion people out of poverty, social injustices still abound, and each year millions of children die from malnutrition and preventable diseases. But despair is unwarranted. The universe cares as much as we do. It has a heart—our very own. We are at once compassionate beings and model builders, the questing knights of Arthurian legend. In that eternal pursuit lies the imperishable dignity of humankind.

THE STEALTH REVOLUTION 12

HAVE PATIENCE WITH EVERYTHING UNRESOLVED IN YOUR HEART AND TRY
TO LOVE *THE QUESTIONS THEMSELVES*. . . . LIVE THE QUESTIONS NOW.
PERHAPS THEN, SOMEDAY FAR IN THE FUTURE, YOU WILL GRADUALLY,
WITHOUT EVEN NOTICING IT, LIVE YOUR WAY INTO THE ANSWER.
—RAINER MARIA RILKE, GERMAN POET

IT'S IMPOSSIBLE TO FORESEE exactly when one social consensus will give way to another. Even after the fact, it's impossible to put your finger on precisely when this happens. Some would argue that the assassination of Martin Luther King, Jr. in 1968 marked such a tipping point with regard to race in the United States; others would say the revolution pivoted on the passing of the civil and voting rights acts. But although not everyone agrees on exactly when it occurred, few dispute that sometime around 1970, America and the rest of the world underwent a profound social transformation. The sixties grip the imagination because they mark the onset of the collapse of the prevailing social contract on race, gender, age, disability, and sexual orientation.

Stories in this book suggest that the dignity movement is already under way and quietly gathering momentum. As a dignitarian culture forms in the crevices and shadows of the current social consensus and institutions restructure themselves, another tipping point approaches. When will it be reached? Ten years from now? Fifty? No one can say. With prior movements, there were decades when nothing seemed to be happening and then, without any perceivable warning, weeks of momentous change. Most movements begin stealthily, and the one for dignity is no exception. But in due course, all of them end up in our face. One day, not too long from now, the dignity movement will be equally plain to see.

A Cautionary Note

Of course, when set beside current events, the model of a dignitarian society drawn in these pages may very well sound utopian. Emerging social models always do until moments before a new consensus displaces a prevailing one. As it turned out, King's "I have a dream" speech was not a pipe dream. It was a timely prophecy of America's imminent emergence as a multicultural society, with global ramifications as well.

As a counterweight to long-range optimism, however, a dollop of short-run pessimism is prudent. A sober assessment of the prospects for a dignitarian society must acknowledge two things. First, in the event of a natural catastrophe, drastic climate change, pandemic, or the use of weapons of mass destruction, the advent of a dignitarian world will surely be slowed. Depending on the circumstances, the delay could be years, decades, or longer. In a worst-case scenario, all bets are off.

Second, every movement must deal with the reaction of those who believe it to be against their interests. In this case, as it grows in numbers, "nobody liberation"—the movement for dignity—will be opposed by somebodies using all the tactics arrayed against earlier uprisings. These range from ridicule to violent suppression, censorship to sabotage, agents provocateurs, fifth columnists, and co-option. In the end, however, the power elite will lose its will to resist and adopt the "If you can't beat 'em, join 'em" position.

The Long-Range View

A model of the stages through which all movements pass and the response of powerholders at each one is laid out in stunning clarity by Bill Moyer in his classic *Doing Democracy: The MAP Model for Organizing Social Movements*.[1] Moyer's model supports what common sense suggests: as it gains force, the dignity movement will encounter every dirty trick in the book and face every weapon in existing arsenals. My guess is that the opposition will exceed in every aspect that mounted against the civil rights and other liberation movements. Simply said, establishing a dignitarian society will be no tea party.

But nothing can suppress forever the will to dignity, not even the will to power. As asserted in the epigraph that opens this volume, "Dignity is not negotiable." In the long run dignity, like liberty, cannot and will not be denied. Indeed, liberty and dignity go hand in hand and neither will be secure until both of them are.

As dignitarian societies demonstrate greater creativity, productivity, fidelity, resourcefulness, and satisfaction than the alternatives, the ideal of dignity for all will become harder and harder to oppose. In the eighteenth century, few would have foreseen that the United States would turn out to be the beacon of democracy that it became for many during the twentieth. Likewise, it's now difficult to identify which nation will first establish a dignitarian society that the rest of the world will come to emulate.

As has already been pointed out, searching for the one "correct" strategy for the dignity movement is futile. Institutional and cultural change are both essential, and individuals gravitate where they will. It's not uncommon for someone to focus on personal change one day and later pursue organizational reform. Cultural advances prepare the ground for institutional ones, and vice versa.

In addition to cultural and institutional fronts, there are local, national, and international arenas. Rankism exists up and down the ladder, operating between nations in much the same way as it does within them. This book has tried to make the case that tolerating rankism in our national affairs is no less corrosive to the American spirit than was our long, sorry accommodation of racism. As we prune rankism from our domestic institutions, attention will turn to exorcising it from our relationships with other nations. As discussed in chapter 10, we must avoid those behaviors that others experience as attempts to dominate, thereby sparing ourselves "blowback" in the form of terrorism and other untoward reactions. This means systematically identifying and eliminating rankism in relationships with other cultures and nations. There is nothing more important to global peace and prosperity than becoming alert to international rankism in all its forms and weeding them out of national policy.

The ability to carry dignitarian principles beyond national boundaries will be furthered by the development of a national dignitarian culture. This is yet another reason to focus on cultural change in conjunction with institutional reform. It almost never happens that one culture treats another better than it treats itself. Nor is any society inclined to enforce international laws that would criminalize what is in fact common practice among its own citizens.

Absent cultural support, simply having laws on the books is not enough to bring about compliance. Consider the American South after the Civil War. Though there were statutes against vigilante justice, it was virtually impossible to convict a white person of lynching. And since passage of the landmark civil rights legislation of the 1960s, there has been a lot of foot-dragging when it comes to according equal dignity to people of color. Similarly, there has been considerable resistance to complying with the Americans with Disabilities Act of 1990.

But as a dignitarian culture takes hold, this situation will change. When juries become less reluctant to convict executives on charges of corporate corruption, the penalties for defrauding people of billions will no longer be milder than those for petty theft. The public will be more likely to hold celebrities to the same standards as ordinary people, and voters will shoo rankist politicians into retirement.

An example of the interplay between institutional and cultural change can be found in our attitudes toward political correctness. No one defends the use of epithets now deemed politically incorrect, at least not out loud. Yet almost everyone finds people annoying who make a show of enforcing political correctness. That may be because the "PC police," as they are derisively called, sometimes assume a posture of ethical superiority, and we resent the rankism inherent in that stance. It has never been easy for targets of abuse and discrimination to confront their tormentors, and to do so without pulling moral rank on them is doubly difficult.

When formalities and legalities get ahead of popular culture, people continue to have prejudicial thoughts, but they bite their tongues to avoid being caught crossing the PC line. That's not a bad thing. It's what my parents did instinctively with regard to race. My grandparents' generation openly used the n-word but my parents never did—at least not in front of me and my brothers—so we didn't pick it up and have to unlearn it as adults. Political correctness may feel burdensome to the generation under pressure to break old habits, but it can be liberating to the next.

Democracy's Next Step

Right now, dignitarian changes are occurring every day, in every walk of life and in all parts of the world, and people are absorbing them without even noticing. Thousands of workers are standing up to rankism in the workplace and increasing numbers of them are doing so without losing their jobs. Antibullying projects are springing up in schools the world over and antibullying Web sites proliferate. The conviction and incarceration of priests for sexual abuse and executives for corporate misdeeds could herald the beginning of the end for two kinds of rankism that have long been condoned if not encouraged.

To take hold, such changes need the support of a broad dignitarian culture, one that is as different from today's status quo as the current consensus on race is from that of the Jim Crow era. One can't imagine the social changes of recent years apart from cultural milestones like the films *To Kill a Mockingbird, Guess Who's Coming to Dinner?, In the Heat of the Night,* and *To Sir, with Love.* Or television shows such as *All in the Family, The Mary Tyler Moore Show, The Cosby Show,* and *Ellen.*

No society has offered a more stark example of the complementarities of political and cultural change than South Africa. Without Nelson Mandela to personify postapartheid multiculturalism, South Africa's political transformation would most likely have been violent.

Many ordinary people are manifestly dignitarian. They not only take care to protect the dignity of those with whom they interact, but also bear witness to, and protest, the indignities they see around them in the world. Such enlightened individuals correspond to the few whites who spoke out against racial bigotry during the era of segregation. Everyone knows a dignitarian or two and, famous or not, they are treasured. But there are those who still act as if rankism is the norm and an indelible part of human nature. The purpose of this book is both to show that this attitude is unwarranted and to suggest a more effective and fulfilling alternative.

Human beings are model builders. Give us a little time and we're shrewd enough to understand that we can harness more power via cooperation than through domination. We're clever enough to reconcile our partisan political positions within a larger, more effective synthesis. We're wise enough not to impose our personal religious beliefs on others. And we're intelligent enough to discern where our nature, social, and self models apply and where they do not, thereby avoiding fruitless conflicts between religion and science and perilous clashes between one religion and another.

In ever greater numbers, people are standing up for their dignity, and once they're on their feet, it won't be long until they march for justice. Targeting rankism is the conceptual bridge that joins the liberation strategies of identity politics to the age-old quest for equity and justice. Building a dignitarian society is democracy's next evolutionary step.

ALL RISE FOR DIGNITY

IF THERE IS NO STRUGGLE, THERE IS NO PROGRESS.
. . . THIS STRUGGLE MAY BE A MORAL ONE, OR IT MAY BE A PHYSICAL
ONE, AND IT MAY BE BOTH, BUT IT MUST BE A STRUGGLE.
POWER CONCEDES NOTHING WITHOUT A DEMAND.
IT NEVER DID AND IT NEVER WILL.
—FREDERICK DOUGLASS

Getting Started

THE DIGNITY MOVEMENT is in its infancy. Yet for every example described in this book, there are thousands more. Taken together, they illustrate that the place to stand up for dignity is right where you are. For those who are ready to do this, I conclude with a list of some simple suggestions drawn from the full text of this book.

▶ *Break the Taboo on Rank*

If you run an organization, make it safe for everyone involved to question the rightful role of rank, the authority vested in specific positions, and the prerogatives associated with the various gradations of rank. Explain to them that you're not doing this to unleash hostility or incite jealousy, but rather to create fairness, and that this may well take multiple "passes" spread over several years' time. Transparency, particularly in the form of open budgeting, is an invaluable tool for reducing rankism, which thrives in dark places. Freedom to speak up or "blow the whistle" without fear of retaliation is essential to dignitarian organizations. Mutual accountability—everyone to everyone else—is their hallmark.

▶ Understand the Roles of Others and Support Equitable Compensation

Wherever you find yourself in the ranks, take responsibility for knowing what others do and understanding how their job fits into the whole. Then recognize their contributions and support compensation that acknowledges the part they play in fulfilling the organizational mission. There aren't many rules yet for determining the monetary worth of one job as compared to another, but clearly rankist self-dealing over the years has produced a gap between rich and poor that is incompatible with the values of a dignitarian society.

▶ Keep Your Promises to Somebodies and Nobodies Alike

One way to tell if you are using the somebody-nobody distinction invidiously as a rationalization for rankist behavior is to notice to whom you keep your promises. In a post-rankist world, we'd all feel as obliged to keep our promises to those whom we outrank as we do to those who outrank us. If you're not sure you'll keep a promise, don't make it.

▶ Create "Indignity-Free Zones"

Teachers are increasingly sensitive to the harm done to students by indignity. If you're an educator, you can bring this awareness into the open and communicate it to those students whose bullying and humiliation of peers unconsciously mirrors that of adult society. An insult to a student's dignity is more than a mere discourtesy. It's an attack on one's status in the "tribe" and carries the implicit danger of ostracism and exclusion. Status has historically been a matter of life and death and remains a determinant of whether we prosper or decline, so an attack on status is experienced as a threat to survival. Schoolchildren begin the school day by reciting the pledge of allegiance to the flag. Perhaps it should be amended to conclude "with liberty, justice, and dignity for all."

▶ Enlist Your Patients as Partners

If you are a health care provider, you can help your clients make the awkward transition from patients to partners. Ridding health care of its legacy of dehumanization and infantilization is simply good medical practice. You can also insist on respect throughout the organization in which you work. If you are a patient, have compassion for your doctors. It's not easy to give up one's "deity status," and many of them are doing so with remarkable grace. Moreover, remember that they're victims of rankism themselves at the hands of HMOs that often treat them less like the professionals they are and more like pieceworkers on an assembly line.

▶ Recognize That Servers Are People, Too

If you're patronizing a store or restaurant, avoid the mistake of thinking that because "the customer is king" you're allowed to act like a tyrant. The majority of servers and clerks are doing their jobs as best they can, often under trying conditions and a great deal of pressure. If you're a salesperson waiting on a customer whom you find unacceptably rude, you may be able to persuade your boss to back you in refusing service. The halo goes to the clerk or salesperson who can devise a dialogue that will induce rankist customers to become aware of their own destructive behavior and change their ways.

▶ Be Aware That Rankism Begets Rankism

If you humiliate those who are abusing rank, they're likely to take it out on their subordinates—often, family members—so there will be no net reduction of rankism in the world. If someone insults your dignity, see if you can break the cycle of rankism begetting rankism. Every situation requires a tailor-made solution and they are often hard to devise. Coming up with something after the fact is not in vain. There will almost certainly be a chance to use it on another occasion.

▶ Have Respect for the Other Team

If you're a coach, you can forbid trash talk, on and off the court, among your players and to your opponents. Show your team that they are capable of more—not by humiliating them but by teaching and inspiring them. Rent the 1973 film *Bang the Drum Slowly* and show it to your athletes. Its punch line—"I rag on nobody"—puts it in the anti-rankist hall of fame.

▸ *Exemplify Rather Than Exhort*

If you're a religious leader, you can refrain from pulling "spiritual rank." You can do more for your flock by listening and providing them with a personal example worthy of emulation than you can by invoking higher authority, which is often little more than a claim that God shares your politics. So, too, with other professions.

▸ *Respect Your Children So They Will Be Respectful*

Today's speakable n-word is "nobody." If you're a parent, you can avoid using it in front of your kids. Parents who listen to their children and who don't belittle them or anyone else are preparing their offspring to inhabit a dignitarian world.

▸ *Adopt a "No Nobodies" Policy in the Schools*

Students may want to see if their friends are interested in adopting a schoolwide policy of "No Nobodies." They could make a list of all the forms that "nobodying" takes and see if others will agree to toss them out.

Equally important, however, is having a plan for dealing with slip-ups. Old habits die hard, and how you go about correcting relapses can be trickier than the pronouncement of noble resolutions. Remember, you can't cure rankism with rankism. When somebody nobodies someone else, it won't improve things to shame the perpetrator. To make the transition from a rankist environment to a dignitarian one, you have to protect the dignity of perpetrator and victim alike as new habits are established. So the real meat and potatoes of a "No Nobodies" policy is not the policy itself, but rather securing agreement on what's to be done when violations of it occur, which they most certainly will. For starters, the person who is nobodied can gently describe to the perpetrator how it feels. Doing this periodically in a public forum (in the manner of instructor Stephanie Heuer's "I feel like a nobody when. . . ." exercise described in chapter 5) is a remedy that often suffices to change what is deemed acceptable behavior by the group.

▶ Be a Susan B. Anthony of the Dignity Movement

In the nineteenth century, Susan B. Anthony traveled a million miles by train and gave twenty thousand speeches advocating the enfranchisement of women. Sadly, she did not live to see the success of the suffragette movement she spearheaded—but her image is on the dollar coin!

If you're an organizer, create a chapter of the dignitarian movement in your area. Coordinate with other chapters and make them a national force under a slogan like "No Rankism" or "Dignity for All." Programs to help the poor or end poverty will continue to fall short until those trapped in the underclass have found their voice and together insist on respect and equity. Do what Susan B. Anthony did for women and Rosa Parks and Martin Luther King, Jr. did for African Americans: help the victims of chronic indignity find an effective way to give voice to their plight and change the status quo.

▶ Bring Dignity to Law Enforcement and Conflict

If you're a police officer, protect citizens' dignity as you already protect their lives. If you're a soldier, protect the dignity of your foes, if only because by so doing you're reducing the chance of them seeking revenge.

▶ Show the World Dignity Through Your Profession

If you're an artist, expose rankism; put dignity on exhibit. If you're a philosopher, define dignity. If you're a psychologist, demonstrate the consequences of malrecognition and show us how to heal its wounds. If you're a historian, chronicle the many forms that rankism has assumed over the centuries. If you're an economist, calculate its cumulative impact on social class and the distribution of wealth. If you're a comedian, make us laugh at the double standards that apply to somebodies and nobodies. If you're a filmmaker, give us heroes who overcome rankism without resorting to rankism. If you're a songwriter, write an anthem for the dignity movement. If you're a TV producer, stop exploiting humiliation and celebrating rankism. Sooner than you think, the current staple of TV entertainment—humiliation—is going to play the way racism now does.

▸ *Honor Your Inner Nobody and Your Inner Somebody Alike*

If you're "just" you, don't be ashamed of the nobody within. It's really a genius—at least, it's your genius. Your inner somebody is dependent on it for new ideas, so don't let your somebody put your nobody down. Remind your somebody that despite all the attention it gets, it's a plagiarist and in grave danger of becoming a "smiling public man."[1] Our somebodies are all guilty of stealing intellectual property from our nobodies. Likewise, if you disparage your inner somebody, you're trashing your meal ticket. It's best to remember that your somebody and your nobody thrive or starve together. Their proper relationship is like that of the masculine and feminine principles we carry within us—peaceful coexistence and mutual respect. As our internal nobodies and somebodies make peace and each gets the recognition it deserves, we typically find ourselves better able to extend to others the dignity we're granting ourselves.

▸ *Remove Rankism from Politics*

If you're in electoral politics you can point the way to a dignitarian society, even if your colleagues aren't yet ready to embrace your ideas. Treat your opponents with dignity. Don't sneer, mock, or condescend. Avoid patronizing or posturing. When politicians affect moral superiority, they extend rankism's lease.

Since rankism is an attack on both liberty and dignity, denounce it along with the other isms. Explain to your constituents why you're against it—in all its forms—and then go after them one by one. Be the leader you wanted to be when you first imagined running for office. Be willing to lose an election for your dignitarian convictions. If you do, run for office a few years later, and win!

To paraphrase Victor Hugo, dignity is an idea whose time has come.

Notes

INTRODUCTION

1. Robert W. Fuller, *Somebodies and Nobodies: Overcoming the Abuse of Rank* (Gabriola Island, British Columbia: New Society Publishers, 2003).
2. "R-E-S-P-E-C-T," *O, The Oprah Magazine*, Apr. 2003, p. 196.
3. *Ableism* is used, alternatively, to refer to the fear of people with disabilities—analogously to *homophobia*—and also to the abuse and discrimination they are the targets of.
4. Betty Friedan, *The Feminine Mystique* (New York: Norton, [1963]1997), p. 15.
5. Thanks to Eileen Hammer for bringing this analogy to my attention.
6. Alexis de Tocqueville, *Democracy in America* (New York: Harper & Row/Perennial Library, 1988), Vol. II, Part IV, ch. 6.
7. For example, John Rawls, *A Theory of Justice* (Cambridge, Mass.: Belknap Press, 1999), Michael Walzer, *Spheres of Justice* (New York: Basic Books, 1983), and Avishai Margalit, *The Decent Society* (Cambridge, Mass.: Harvard University Press, 1996).

CHAPTER 1

1. Jim Yardley, "Rape in China: A Nightmare for 26 Pupils," *New York Times*, June 21, 2005, p. 1.
2. John Sullivan, "Nuclear Plant in New Jersey Draws Censure," *New York Times*, Oct. 21, 2005, p. A1.
3. Gen. 1:26.
4. See, for example, Carolyn Merchant, *Reinventing Eden: The Fate of Western Culture* (New York: Routledge, 2003).

CHAPTER 2

1. Garry Wills, *Lincoln at Gettysburg: The Words That Remade America* (New York: Simon & Schuster, 1993).
2. The word *dignity* has been given a variety of meanings over the centuries. An excellent account of these meanings is provided by Gabriel Moran, professor of religious studies at New York University, in his essays on dignity, uniqueness, and rights. Another illuminating discussion of the meaning of dignity appears in Margalit's insightful study, *The Decent Society*. Finally, *dignity* has provoked an intense

discussion in the context of medical ethics. A sample can be found at http://bmj.bmjjournals.com/cgi/eletters/327/7429/1419.

3. See Steven LeBlanc and Katherine E. Register, *Constant Battles: The Myth of the Peaceful, Noble Savage* (New York: St. Martin's Press, 2003).

4. For example, Article 1 of the Basic Law for the Federal Republic of Germany reads: "Human dignity shall be inviolable. To respect and protect it shall be the duty of all state authority."

5. William Shakespeare, *Merchant of Venice*, 3.1.52–53.

6. Sojourner Truth, address to the Ohio Women's Rights Conference, Akron, May 29, 1851. In Deirdre Mullane, *Words to Make My Dream Children Live: A Book of African American Quotations* (New York: Anchor, 1995), p. 430.

7. Shakespeare, *Merchant of Venice*, 3.1.63–65.

8. As quoted by Harvey J. Kaye in *Thomas Paine and the Promise of America* (New York: Hill & Wang, 2005), p. 200.

9. *BBC News*, May 14, 2005; see http://news.bbc.co.uk/2/hi/europe/4547227.stm.

10. See, for example, Jeffrey D. Sachs and Pedro A. Sanchez, "We Can End World Hunger," *World Arc*, Nov./Dec. 2004. Also see Jeffrey Sachs, *The End of Poverty: Economic Possibilities for Our Time* (New York: Penguin Books, 2005).

11. You can learn about the Center for Therapeutic Justice at www.therapeuticjustice .com. Also, see the cover story in *American Jails*, Jan./Feb. 2006: "Center for Therapeutic Justice's Community Model: The Jail Administrator's Best Friend—Security Friendly Programming," Vol XIX, No. 6, p. 35. Visit the Centre for Restorative Justice at www.sfu.ca/crj for a model that emphasizes rehabilitation instead of punishment. Also see Alan Elsner's book, *Gates of Injustice: The Crisis in America's Prisons* (Englewood Cliffs, N.J.: Financial Times/Prentice Hall, 2004).

12. Claire Sheridan, personal communication with the author, Oct. 21, 2005.

13. Noah Brand, personal communication with the author, Oct. 4, 2005.

14. See www.hyperhistory.net/apwh/bios/b2archimedes_p1ab.htm.

15. Lani Guinier, Harvard Law School professor and author of many books and articles on race and gender equity, describes allies who, regardless of color, align themselves with the rights of subalterns seeking inclusion as being "politically black." See Lani Guinier, *The Miner's Canary: Rethinking Race and Power* (Cambridge, Mass.: Harvard University Press, 2002).

16. Richard E. Baldwin, writer and realtor, personal communication with the author, Oct. 2005.

CHAPTER 3

1. A book is devoted to explicating the Leon Lederman remark: Don Falk, *Universe on a T-Shirt: The Quest for the Theory of Everything* (Canada: Penguin Books, 2004). There is also one coauthored by Lederman himself: Leon M. Lederman and Christopher T. Hill, *Symmetry and the Beautiful Universe* (Amherst, N.Y.: Prometheus Books, 2004).

2. An excellent and accessible description of string theory can be found in *The Elegant Universe* by Brian Greene (New York: Vintage, 2000); see also Greene's *The Fabric of the Cosmos* (New York: Knopf, 2004).

3. Edmund L. Andrews, "The Doctrine Was Not to Have One; Greenspan Will Leave No Road Map to His Successor," *New York Times*, Aug. 26, 2005, p. C1.

4. For Bertrand Russell quote, see http://en.proverbia.net/citasautor.asp?autor= 16327&page=11.

5. For Galileo recantation, see www.law.umkc.edu/faculty/projects/ftrials/galileo/recantation.html.

6. Walter Truett Anderson discusses the evolving meaning of the truth in his book *The Truth About the Truth: De-Confusing and Re-Constructing the Postmodern World* (New York: Tarcher, 1995).

7. Freeman Dyson, *Infinite in All Directions* (New York: HarperPerennial, 2004).

8. Stephanie Coontz, *Marriage, a History: From Obedience to Intimacy, or How Love Conquered Marriage* (New York: Viking, 2005).

9. Statistics from Gwynne Dyer, London-based syndicated columnist, in a column circulated by Global Business Network under the title *Global Perspectives*, Sept. 26, 2005.

10. Enrico Fermi, "The Future of Nuclear Physics," unpublished address, Rochester, New York, Jan. 10, 1953. In *Proceedings of the International Conference*, "Enrico Fermi and the Universe of Physics," Rome, Sept. 29–Oct. 2, 2001 (Rome: Accademia Nazionale dei Lincei, Istituto Nazionale de Fisica Nucleare, ENEA, 2003).

11. Stewart Brand, editor of the *Whole Earth Catalog* (Menlo Park, Calif.: Portola Institute, 1968–71; New York: Viking, 1972; New York: Random House, 1980–81; New York: Doubleday, 1988) and author of *Clock of the Long Now* (New York: Basic Books, 1999).

12. The practice of conducting such thought-experiments—often called by their German name *Gedankenexperiments*—is part of every physicist's training.

13. For the Clement Attlee quote, see www.creativequotations.com/one/1705.htm.

CHAPTER 4

1. Jim Collins, *Good to Great: Why Some Companies Make the Leap . . . and Others Don't* (New York: HarperCollins, 2001).

2. Robert Knisely, "Rank Prejudice," *Washington Monthly*, Apr. 2003, pp. 59–60. In *Good to Great*, Collins provides a quantitative definition of "exceptional performance" in terms of cumulative stock returns.

3. Noel Hinners, personal communication with the author, Apr. 8, 2005.

4. During the nuclear arms race of the cold war, political activist Fran Peavey sat on park benches in various international capitals with a sign reading "American Willing to Listen." She describes the effects of doing this in her book *Heart Politics* (Montreal: Black Rose Books, 1985).

5. In a personal e-mail to me. The teacher involved asked for anonymity for all concerned.

6. For more on Google's culture, visit www.google.com/corporate/culture.html.

7. For the Hyman Rickover quote, see, for example, www.pillowrock.com/ronnie /responsibility.htm. See also the statement of Admiral F. L. "Skip" Bowman, director, Naval Nuclear Propulsion Program, U.S. Navy, before the House Committee on Science, Oct. 20, 2003.

8. See http://66.102.7.104/search?q=cache:voKAY85bpNwJ:www.winus.org/documents /GehmanInterview.pdf+%22commander+aviator%22&hl=en to read the interview with Hal Gehman.

9. Daniel McGinn, "The Green Machine," *Newsweek,* Mar. 21, 2005, pp. E8–12.

10. Dennis Bakke, *Joy at Work: A Revolutionary Approach to Fun on the Job* (Frankfurt, Germany: PVG, 2005).

11. "Breakthrough Ideas for 2005," *Harvard Business Review,* Feb. 2005. The list is an annual survey of emerging management ideas.

12. Gerard Fairtlough, *The Three Ways of Getting Things Done: Hierarchy, Heterarchy, and Responsible Autonomy in Organizations* (Greenways, Ryall, Dorset, U.K.: Triarchy Press, 2005). Heterarchy means multiple or dispersed rule and a balance of power, with no one person or group dominant, rather than the single rule of hierarchy. In a heterarchy, decisions are reached by dialogue rather than dictate.

13. Art Kleiner, "Diversity and Its Discontents," *Strategy + Business,* spring 2004; see www.well.com/~art/sbspr2004cc.htm.

14. Dr. Thomas made these remarks at the City Club of Cleveland Forum, Sept. 30, 2005. See also David A. Thomas and John J. Gabarro, *Breaking Through: The Making of Minority Executives in Corporate America* (Cambridge, Mass.: Harvard Business School Press, 1999).

15. Wes Boyd, e-mail communication with the author, Oct. 3, 2005.

16. Michel Bauwens, "P2P and Human Evolution: Peer-to-Peer as the Premise of a New Mode of Civilization." See www.networkcultures.org/weblog/archives /P2P_essay.pdf#search='p2p%20and%20human%20evolution.

17. Regarding the open source movement generally, see Steven Weber, *The Success of Open Source* (Cambridge, Mass.: Harvard University Press, 2004). More on collaborative peer production can be found in Yochai Benkler, "Coase's Penguin, or Linux and the Nature of the Firm," *Yale Law Journal.* See www.yale.edu/yalelj/112 /BenklerWEB .pdf.

18. See Samuel E. Finer, *The History of Government* (Oxford: Oxford University Press, 1997). See also http://wikipedia.org/wiki/klerostocracy.

19. Bulleted items excerpted and paraphrased from the Acorn Center's Web site at www.workthatworks.ca. In addition to Dr. Levey and Dr. Morrill, who are noted in the text extract, Acorn acknowledges www.workdoctor.com, Dr. Harvey Hornstein, author of *Brutal Bosses and Their Prey* (New York: Riverhead Press, 1997), and an article by Benedict Carey in the *New York Times* that was reprinted in the *Toronto*

Star on July 2, 2004. The entire Acorn Center article can be found at http://work-thatworks.ca/editorials.php?section=opinion.

20. John M. McCardell, Jr., "What Your College President Didn't Tell You," *New York Times*, Sept. 13, 2004, op-ed page.

21. For example, an article in the *New York Times* (Eric Nagourney, "Vital Signs: Injustices at Work May Harm Men's Hearts," Nov. 1, 2005, p. F6) reports that "a Finnish study, published Oct. 24, 2005 in *Archives of Internal Medicine*, [shows that] men who perceived a low level of justice at work were more likely to suffer angina, heart attack, or death from coronary artery disease than those who perceived a high level of justice."

22. For more information on the LEAP program, visit www.stmarys-ca.edu/academics /adult_graduate/programs_by_school/school_of_extended_education/programs /leap/.

CHAPTER 5

1. Susan Faludi, *Backlash: The Undeclared War Against American Women* (New York: Anchor, 1992).

2. As reported on NPR's *Talk of the Nation* on June 8, 2005; see www.npr.org/tem-plates /story/story.php?storyId=4694537. The works of Jonathan Kozol and Parker Palmer are excellent sources on the signal importance of respecting those we teach—and on what doing so in the classroom really means.

3. E-mail communication with the author, Oct. 2, 2005.

4. For example, see Michael B. Katz, *Class, Bureaucracy, and Schools: The Illusion of Educational Change in America* (New York: Praeger, 1975).

5. Julie Bosman, "Putting the Gym Back in Gym Class," *New York Times*, Oct. 13, 2005.

6. These statistics are from a 2005 exhibit on bullying in schools supported by the Logan Family Fund and held at the Addison Street Windows Gallery in Berkeley, California. See J. Douglas Allen-Taylor, "Middle School Students Tackle Bullying In Addison Street Windows Poster Display," *Berkeley Daily Planet*, Feb. 1, 2005.

7. Rosalind Wiseman, *Queen Bees and Wannabes: Helping Your Daughter Survive Cliques, Gossip, Boyfriends, and Other Realities of Adolescence* (New York: Three Rivers Press, 2003); Rachel Simmons, *Odd Girl Out: The Hidden Culture of Aggression in Girls* (New York: Harvest Books, 2003).

8. You can reach Youth Empowering Systems at P.O. Box 1335, Sebastopol, Calif. 95473, or visit www.nta-ycs.com or call 800/624-1120.

9. Lauren Collins, "Don't Laugh," *The New Yorker*, July 4, 2005, pp. 31–32.

10. Visit Operation Respect at www.dontlaugh.org. The lyrics to *Don't Laugh at Me* are available at http://pages.zdnet.com/ourorhskids/id65.html.

11. Stephen Potter, *One-Upmanship* (Kingston, R.I.: Asphodel Press, [1952]1997).

12. Allyn Jackson, "As If Summoned from the Void: The Life of Alexandre Grothen-dieck," *Notices of the American Mathematical Society*, 51(10), pp. 1196–1216.

13. Paul R. Halmos, *Finite Dimensional Vector Spaces* (New York: Springer, 1993).

14. In a piece titled "True Story: The Art of Short Fiction," in the Dec. 1, 2003 issue of the *New Yorker* (p. 105), Louis Menand discusses James Joyce's use of the word *epiphany* in a literary context: "What Joyce meant by an epiphany was, he said, just 'a revelation of the whatness of a thing'—a sudden apprehension of the way the world unmediatedly is. Language being one of the principal means by which the world is mediated, the epiphany is an experience beyond (or after, or without) words."

Chapter 6

1. The evocative term "MDeity" was coined by writer Anna Quindlan.

2. Lindsey Tanner, "Apology a Tool to Avoid Malpractice," *Boston Globe*, Nov. 12, 2004.

3. See C. M. Clark, "Incivility in Nursing Education: Student Perceptions of Uncivil Faculty Behaviors in the Academic Environment," *Dissertation Abstracts International*, forthcoming.

4. Abigail Zuger, M.D., "Defining a Doctor, With a Tear, a Shrug and a Schedule," *New York Times*, Nov. 2, 2004.

5. Helen Epstein, "Enough to Make You Sick," *New York Times Magazine*, Oct. 12, 2003, p. 74. The link between heart disease and working conditions is reported in an article by Amanda Gardner, "Don't Work Your Heart Out," *HealthDay Reporter*, Oct. 24, 2005; see http://bullyinginstitute.org/res/justiceheart2.html. In the nineteenth century, "childbed fever" killed many new mothers. This mysterious "miasma" was finally understood by the Hungarian obstetrician Ignac Semmelweiss as resulting from microbes transmitted by unhygienic conditions in hospitals—not least of which was the unwashed hands of the doctors themselves. The "new ghetto miasma" described in the *New York Times Magazine* likewise has an invisible cause—rankism, in the language of this book—but this time, guilt cannot be laid at the hands of doctors but rather at society's.

6. CBS News broadcast this story in Toronto, Canada, on Feb. 26, 2005; see www.cbsnews.com/stories/2005/02/26/oscar/printable676686.shtml.

7. "How Social Status Affects Our Health," *San Francisco Chronicle*, Aug. 1, 2004, p. E3.

8. Ibid.

9. Michael Marmot, "Life at the Top," *New York Times*, Feb. 27, 2005, op-ed page. See also Robert M. Sapolsky, "The Influence of Social Hierarchy on Primate Health," *Science*, Apr. 29, 2005, p. 648.

10. For more information on this project, see Search for Common Ground's Web site at www.sfcg.org.

11. Thomas A. Purvis, e-mail communication with the author, Oct. 20, 2005.

12. Richard Pérez-Peña, "At Clinic, Hurdles to Clear Before Medicaid Care," *New York Times*, Oct. 17, 2005, p. A1.

CHAPTER 7

1. Barbara Ehrenreich, *Nickel and Dimed: On (Not) Getting By in America* (New York: Owl Books, 2002).

2. David Shipler, *The Working Poor: Invisible in America* (New York: Knopf, 2004).

3. Howard Karger, *Shortchanged: Life and Debt in the Fringe Economy* (San Francisco: Berrett-Koehler, 2005). See, for example, pp. 97–99.

4. The student who made this demand was Meg Root.

5. Thomas Paine's proposals for a "national fund" that would compensate the landless and dispossessed "on every principle of justice, of gratitude, and of civilization" can be found in his book *Agrarian Justice* (1797). See Philip Foner, *The Complete Works of Thomas Paine, Vol. 1* (New York: Citadel Press, 1945), pp. 612–613, 620. A summary is provided in Harvey J. Kaye's biography *Thomas Paine and the Promise of America* (New York: Hill & Wang, 2005).

6. Richard E. Baldwin, *Re-Birth of A Nation: American Identity and the Culture Wars* (forthcoming); Michael Sherraden, *Assets and the Poor* (Armonk, N.Y.: Sharpe, 1991); Bruce A. Ackerman and Anne Alstott, *The Stakeholder Society* (New Haven, Conn.: Yale University Press, 1999); Jonathon Rowe, "Every Baby a Trust Fund Baby," *American Prospect,* Jan. 2001.

7. Richard E. Baldwin, e-mail communication with the author, May 28, 2005.

8. "The Economic Bill of Rights," which warrants comparison with the dignitarian agenda presented in this chapter and the next, was proposed to the U.S. Congress by President Franklin D. Roosevelt in his Jan. 11, 1944 State of the Union Address. See www.worldpolicy.org/globalrights/econrights/fdr-econbill.html.

CHAPTER 8

1. For example, Riane Eisler, *The Chalice and the Blade: Our History, Our Future* (San Francisco: HarperCollins, 1987), and Robert Wright, *Non-Zero: The Logic of Human Destiny* (New York: Pantheon, 2000).

2. See Greg Palast, *The Best Democracy Money Can Buy* (New York: Plume, 2004).

3. Benedict Carey, "Some Politics May Be Etched in the Genes," *New York Times,* June 21, 2005, p. F1.

4. George Lakoff, *Moral Politics: What Conservatives Know That Liberals Don't* (Chicago: University of Chicago Press, 1996).

5. Linda B. Major, *Dramatic Search for Root of Chicanismo* (San Juan Bautista, Calif.: Guaracha Publications, summer 1974), p. 7. Thanks to Linne Gravestock for providing this aphorism.

6. See www.transpartisan.net for more on this concept.

7. Shelley L. Davis, *Unbridled Power: Inside the Secret Culture of the IRS* (New York: HarperBusiness, 1997). See also the 1997 testimony by Senator Wayne Allard to the full U.S. Senate on the IRS at http://allard.senate.gov/issues/item.cfm?id =488&rands _type=3.

CHAPTER 9

1. Michael Kimmelman, "Kirk Varnedoe, 57, Curator Who Changed the Modern's Collection and Thinking, Dies," *New York Times,* Aug 15, 2003.

2. Betsy Leondar-Wright, *Class Matters* (Gabriola Island, British Columbia: New Society Publishers, 2005).

3. William Shakespeare, *Measure for Measure,* 2.2.118–123. This passage was brought to my attention by Douglas Harding, whose book *On Having No Head* (London: Inner Directions Foundation, [1961]2002) is an eye-opener. It is regarded as a modern spiritual classic.

4. The full passage is one of the most powerful testaments to dignity in American literature: "I don't say he's a great man. Willy Loman never made a lot of money. His name was never in the paper. He's not the finest character that ever lived. But he's a human being, and a terrible thing is happening to him. So attention must be paid. He's not to be allowed to fall into this grave like an old dog. Attention, attention must be finally paid to such a person." Arthur Miller, *Death of a Salesman* (New York City: Penguin, [1949]1998).

5. David Mamet eulogized Arthur Miller in his piece "Attention Must Be Paid," *New York Times,* Feb. 14, 2005, op-ed page.

6. William Shakespeare, *As You Like It,* 2.7.138–141. "All the world's a stage/And all the men and women merely players/They have their exits and their entrances/And one man in his time plays many parts."

7. *The Human Comedy* is the collective title of the gargantuan cycle of linked stories and novels written by nineteenth-century French author Honoré de Balzac, who shared Shakespeare's witnessing perspective, and in that spirit, saw life as a parade. In his collection of stories *Wineburg, Ohio* (New York: Penguin Books, [1919]1992), Sherwood Anderson evinces a similar enlightened perspective.

8. Harold Bloom, *The Western Canon* (Orlando: Harcourt Brace, 1994).

9. See www.jafi.org.il/education/hartman/4quest.html.

10. In *The Book of Laughter and Forgetting* (New York: Penguin Books, 1981), Czechoslovakian-born novelist Milan Kundera echoes Wallace Stegner: "A novel poses questions. . . . The stupidity of people comes from having an answer for everything. The wisdom of a novel comes from having a question for everything" (p. 237).

11. The English poet Stephen Spender wrote in his autobiographical novel *World Within World* (London: Reader's Union Ltd., 1953): "So I clung to my belief in myself but kept it a secret. . . . My 'extraordinariness,' did not lie in my being exceptionally clever or even gifted. It lay in a strong grasp of my uniqueness in time and space. I was aware that I was different from everyone else in the same sense in which everyone is different from everyone else" (p. 35).

12. Carolyn G. Heilbrun, *Writing a Woman's Life* (New York: Ballantine Books, 1989).

13. See www.parkwestgallery.com/invites/Chagall.pdf.

14. This quotation is the translation of William Arrowsmith, who supplied it in a personal communication to the author.

15. Henry James, "The Art of Fiction," in *Partial Portraits* (New York: Macmillan, 1888); see http://guweb2.gonzaga.edu/faculty/campbell/engl462/artfiction.html.

16. See www.john-keats.com/briefe/221117.htm

17. Martin Buber, *The Way of Man According to the Teaching of Hasidism* (New York: Citadel Press, 1995), p. 17.

18. For a philosophy of improvisation that goes far beyond stage use, see Keith John-stone's classic *Impro: Improvisation and the Theatre* (New York: Routledge, 1979).

19. Ray Kurzweil, *The Singularity Is Near: When Humans Transcend Biology* (New York: Viking, 2005). See also Joel Garreau, *Radical Evolution: The Promise and Peril of Enhancing Our Minds, Our Bodies—And What It Means to Be Human* (New York: Doubleday, 2005).

CHAPTER 10

1. Langston Hughes's 1922 volume entitled *The Weary Blues* included this poem: "I've got the Weary Blues/And I can't be satisfied . . . /I ain't happy no mo'/And I wish that I had died." The British dramatist and composer Noël Coward applied Hughes's phrase to the collective travails of his time: "I got those weary twentieth-century blues." In 1980 David Hoffman, president of the organization Internews, which promotes free media around the world, coined the phrase "evolutionary blues" to highlight the fact that human angst is in part a species-wide coming-of-age phenomenon. He used it as the title of his journal, which was published as a response to the perils of the nuclear arms race. See www.biblio.com/details.php?dcx=28227497&src=frg.

2. H. G. Wells, *The Outline of History* (New York, Doubleday, [1920]1971).

3. See Mark Gerzon, *Leading Through Conflict: How Successful Leaders Transform Differences into Opportunity* (Cambridge, Mass.: Harvard Business School Press, 2006).

4. John Fowles, *Daniel Martin* (Boston: Little, Brown, 1977).

5. An article in the first issue of *Evolutionary Blues*, titled "A Better Game Than War," is based on editor David Hoffman's interview of the author. See www.context.org/ICLIB/IC04/Fuller.htm.

6. For statistics on frequency and duration of wars, see www.user.erols.com/mwhite28/war-1900.htm. Also, the authoritative Stockholm International Peace Research Institute, in a 2004 report, said that nineteen major armed conflicts were under way worldwide the previous year, a sharp drop from the thirty-three counted in 1991 (see www.taipeitimes.com/News/world/archives/2004/08/30/2003200889). Another report cited in the same *Taipei Times* article estimates battle-related deaths world-wide at fifteen thousand in 2002, and because of the Iraq war, rising to twenty thousand in 2003. Those estimates are down from annual tolls ranging from forty thousand to one hundred thousand in the 1990s and from a post–World War II peak of seven hundred thousand in 1951. See also users.erols.com/mwhite28/war-1900.htm.

7. See, for example, Robert Pape, *Dying to Win: The Strategic Logic of Suicide Terrorism* (New York: Random House, 2005). Page argues that religious fundamentalism
is rarely the root cause of suicidal terrorism. More often, terrorists have secular,
strategic goals based on a desire to expel occupiers from land they regard as rightfully theirs. Other sources on this subject are Bernard Lewis, *The Crisis of Islam:
Holy War and Unholy Terror* (New York: Modern Library, 2003); Paul Berman, *Terror and Liberalism* (New York: Norton, 2003); and Jessica Stern, *Terror in the Name
of God: Why Religious Militants Kill* (New York: Ecco, 2003). Stern, who interviewed
seventy-five terrorists around the world, argues that a common thread in their
accounts is humiliation. She says, "For most Islamist groups, they feel that Islamic
civilization has fallen behind politically, economically, intellectually and that is
deeply humiliating, and someone is to blame." Among American terrorists, humiliation is often based on personal experience. Stern writes of an American terrorist, for example, who described himself as being sickly as a boy and placed in the
girls' gym class.
8. See the section on peer-to-peer (P2P) organizations in chapter 4.
9. Thomas Friedman, "Rooting Out the Jihadist Cancer," *New York Times,* July 8, 2005,
op-ed page. For more on the subject of shame, see John Bradshaw, *Healing the
Shame That Binds You* (Deerfield Beach, Fla.: HCI, 1988).
10. Many have written about how Germany's humiliation in the aftermath of World
War I was one of the causes of World War II. For example, see Evelin Gerda Lindner, *Making Enemies Unwittingly: Humiliation and International Conflict* (Westport, Conn.: Praeger, 2006), and also the Web site of Human Dignity and
Humiliation Studies at www.humiliationstudies.org.
11. SWAT is an acronym for Special Weapons and Tactics. For more on standoffs and
the response to them, see the work by sociologist Robin Wagner-Pacifici, *Theoriz-
ing the Standoff: Contingency in Action* (Cambridge, U.K.: Cambridge University
Press, 2000).

CHAPTER 11

1. Samuel P. Huntington, *The Clash of Civilizations and the Remaking of the World
Order* (New York: Simon & Schuster, 1998).
2. Tenzin Gyatso, the Dalai Lama, "Our Faith in Science," *New York Times,* Nov. 12,
2005, p. A15.
3. Mo-tzu lived and practiced his own brand of citizen diplomacy in the fifth century
BCE in China. He is less well-known in the West than other prophets, but no less
significant. He may have been the first person to see the world as a village of kin-
folk and therefore to realize that offensive war is never justified. His doctrine of universal love was far ahead of its time, and his reputation was soon eclipsed by the
more down-to-earth Confucius. An introduction to his thought is provided by
Burton Watson in *Mo Tzu: Basic Writings* (New York: Columbia University Press,

1963). Sankara was an Indian philosopher of Advaita Vedanta who lived in the eighth century CE.

4. William Golding, *Lord of the Flies* (New York: Berkeley Books, 1959).

5. Works that explore the self and its transformation include the plays of William Shakespeare, Dante's *Divine Comedy*, Cervantes' *Don Quixote*, Milton's *Paradise Lost*, Melville's *Moby Dick*, and Dostoevky's *Brothers Karamazov*.

CHAPTER 12

1. Bill Moyer, *Doing Democracy: The MAP Model for Organizing Social Movements* (Gabriola Island, British Columbia: New Society Publishers, 2001).

AFTERWORD

1. From the W. B. Yeats poem, "Among School Children." See, for example, *The Collected Poems of W. B. Yeats* (New York: Macmillan, 1972), pp. 212–213. The first stanza concludes as follows: "The children learn to cipher and to sing/To study reading-books and history/To cut and sew, be neat in everything/In the best modern way—the children's eyes/In momentary wonder stare upon/A sixty-year-old smiling public man."

ACKNOWLEDGMENTS

1. Peter A. Putnam (1926–1987) published only a few papers, although his private writings were voluminous. Some of them are housed in the library of Union Theological Seminary in New York City. Others can be found at the Web site www.peterputnam.org. In 1967, Wesleyan University Press published a much earlier version of the material on values that appears here in chapter 11. It was titled "Causal and Moral Law—Their Relationship as Examined in Terms of a Model of the Brain" and appeared as no. 13 in a series of Monday Evening Papers presented at Wesleyan's Center for Advanced Study. A related paper, coauthored with Putnam, which outlines his Darwinian model of brain function, is titled "On the Origin of Order in Behavior." See Ludwig von Bertalanffy and Anatol Rapoport (eds.), *General Systems, Vol. XI* (Ann Arbor: Mental Health Research Institute, University of Michigan, 1966), pp. 99–112.

Resources

THIS SECTION LISTS alphabetically by author some of the resources I've consulted in developing the ideas found in this book. They may prove of interest to readers who want to pursue certain topics in more depth. Books cited in the chapter endnotes may be omitted here.

Books

Anita Allen. *The New Ethics: A Guided Tour of the Twenty-First Century Moral Landscape.* New York: Miramax Books, 2004.

Gar Alperowitz. *America Beyond Capitalism:Reclaiming Our Wealth, Our Liberty and Our Democracy.* New York: Wiley, 2004.

Mark Ames. *Going Postal: Rage, Murder, and Rebellion: From Reagan's Workplaces to Clinton's Columbine and Beyond.* Brooklyn, N.Y.: Soft Skull Press, 2005.

Walter Truett Anderson. *The Next Enlightenment: Integrating East and West in a New Vision of Human Evolution.* New York: St. Martin's Press, 2003.

Kwame Anthony Appiah. *The Ethics of Identity.* Princeton: Princeton University Press, 2004.

Kwame Anthony Appiah. *Cosmopolitanism: Ethics in a World of Strangers.* New York: Norton, 2006.

Daniel Benjamin and Steven Simon. *The Next Attack: The Failure of the War on Terror and a Strategy for Getting It Right.* New York: Times Books/Henry Holt, 2005.

Samuel Bowles, Herbert Gintis, and Melissa Osborne Groves (eds.). *Unequal Chances: Family Background and Economic Success.* Princeton: Princeton University Press, 2005.

George Chauncey. *Gay New York: Gender, Urban Culture, and the Making of the Gay Male World, 1890–1940.* New York: Basic Books, 1995.

Correspondents of the *New York Times. Class Matters.* New York: Times Books/Henry Holt, 2005).

Alain de Botton. *Status Anxiety.* New York: Vintage, 2005.

Gwynne Dyer. *Future Tense: The Coming World Order.* Toronto, Canada: McClelland and Stewart, 2004.

Esther Dyson. *Release 2.1: A Design for Living in the Digital Age.* New York: Broadway Books, 1998.

Edward M. Fergusson. *Jihad the Jerk at Work.* Lake Hiawatha, N.J.: Dunkeld House, 2005.

Robert Frank and Phillip J. Cook. *The Winner-Take-All Society: Why the Few at the Top Get So Much More Than the Rest of Us.* New York: Penguin, 1996.

Vivian Gornick. *The Solitude of Self: Thinking About Elizabeth Cady Stanton.* New York: Farrar, Straus and Giroux, 2005.

Richard Haass. *Intervention: The Use of American Military Force in the Post–Cold War World.* Washington, D.C.: Brookings Institution Press, 1994.

Morton H. Halperin. *The Democracy Advantage: How Democracies Promote Prosperity and Peace.* Oxford: Routledge, 2004.

Chauncey Hare and Judith Wyatt. *Work Abuse: How to Recognize and Survive It.* Rochester, Vt.: Schenkman Books, 1997.

Albert O. Hirschman. *Exit, Voice, and Loyalty: Responses to Decline in Firms, Organizations, and States.* Cambridge, Mass.: Harvard University Press, 1970.

Adam Hochschild. *Bury the Chains: Prophets and Rebels in the Fight to Free an Empire's Slaves.* Boston: Houghton Mifflin, 2005.

Mary Johnson. *Make Them Go Away: Clint Eastwood, Christopher Reeve & the Case Against Disability Rights.* Louisville, Ky.: Advocado Press, 2003.

Paul W. Kingston. *The Classless Society.* Palo Alto: Stanford University Press, 2000.

Art Kleiner. *Who Really Matters: The Core Group Theory of Power, Privilege, and Success.* New York: Doubleday, 2003.

Brad Land. *Goat.* New York: Random House, 2004.

Annette Lareau. *Unequal Childhoods: Class, Race, and Family Life.* Berkeley: University of California Press, 2003.

Sara Lawrence-Lightfoot. *Respect: An Exploration.* New York: Perseus Books, 2000.

Evelin Gerda Lindner. *Making Enemies Unwittingly: Humiliation and International Conflict.* Westport, Conn.: Praeger, 2006.

S. M. Miller and Anthony J. Savoie. *Respect and Rights: Class, Race, and Gender Today.* Lanham, Md.: Rowman & Littlefield, 2002.

Martha C. Nussbaum. *Frontiers of Justice: Disability, Nationality, Species Membership.* Cambridge, Mass.: Belknap Press, 2006.

Jay Ogilvy. *Many Dimensional Man: Decentralizing Self, Society, and the Sacred.* Oxford: Oxford University Press, 1971.

Kevin Phillips. *Wealth and Democracy: A Political History of the American Rich.* New York: Broadway Books, 2003.

Sam Roberts. *Who We Are Now: The Changing Face of America in the 21st Century.* New York: Times Books, 2004.

Marc Sageman. *Understanding Terror Networks.* Philadelphia: University of Pennsylvania Press, 2004.

James C. Scott. *Weapons of the Weak: Everyday Forms of Peasant Resistance.* New Haven: Yale University Press, 1985.

Richard Sennett. *Respect in a World of Inequality.* New York: Norton, 2003.

Beth Shulman. *The Betrayal of Work: How Low-Wage Jobs Fail 30 Million Americans and Their Families.* New York: New Press, 2003.

William Talbott. *Which Human Rights Should Be Universal?* Oxford: Oxford University Press, 2005.

Charles Taylor. *Philosophical Arguments.* Cambridge, Mass.: Harvard University Press, 1995.

William H. Thomas. *What Are Old People For? How Elders Will Save the World.* Acton, Mass.: Vanderwyk & Burnham, 2004.

Mark Twain. *What Is Man?* Los Angeles: Green Integer, 2000.

Jim Wallis. *God's Politics: Why the Right Gets It Wrong and the Left Doesn't Get It.* San Francisco: HarperCollins, 2005.

Michael Walzer. *Arguing About War.* New Haven, Conn.: Yale University Press, 2004.

Julie Wambach. *Battles Among Somebodies and Nobodies: Stop Abuse of Rank in Your Personal, Professional, and Public Lives.* Forthcoming.

Rosalind Wiseman, *Queen Bees and Wannabes,* New York: Three Rivers Press, 2003; and *Queen Bee Moms and Kingpin Dads,* New York: Crown, 2006.

Kenji Yoshino. *Covering: The Hidden Assault on our Civil Rights.* New York: Random House, 2006.

Web Sites

Tim Field. Bully Online: www.bullyonline.org

Tim Field. Success Unlimited: www.successunlimited.co.uk

Robert W. Fuller. Breaking Ranks: www.breakingranks.net

Chauncey Hare and Judith Wyatt. Work and Family Resources: www.home.netcom.com/~workfam1/

Mary Johnson. Ragged Edge Online: www.ragged-edge-mag.com

Evelin Gerda Lindner. Human Dignity and Humiliation Studies: http://humiliationstudies.org

Joseph McCormick. Transpartisan News: www.transpartisan.net

Peter A. Putnam: www.peterputnam.org

Ann Richardson and Mary Lou Richardson. Dignitarian Foundation: www.dignitarians.org

Julie Wambach. Right-rank: www.right-rank.com

Acknowledgments

THIS BOOK WOULD NOT EXIST but for its predecessor, *Somebodies and Nobodies*, which was made possible by the unfailing trust and support of Robert Cabot. Thanks are also due to the late Bill Moyer, who brought that manuscript to the attention of New Society Publishers. Additionally, the innovative marketing strategy devised by Ruth Ann Harnisch, and the support of the Harnisch Family Foundation, greatly extended the reach of the volume's core ideas—rankism and a dignitarian society to overcome it—and thereby helped create the need for this sequel.

Like its predecessor, *All Rise* draws on hundreds of interactions stretching over decades. A sizable number of contributions came from strangers who wrote me with suggestions, cases in point, and anguished tales of what rankism had wrought in their lives. Quite a few of these stories have found their way into this book. I have tried to credit every contributor and paraphrase their words accurately. It is never my intention to appropriate others' work without proper acknowledgment, but in a broad project of this nature I realize there may well be oversights. For them, I apologize, and if notified, will amend subsequent editions.

Contributors to the project include Laura Adams, Walter Truett Anderson, Jonathan Arms, John Atkins, Andrea Ayvasian, Richard Baldwin, Bill Benda, Peter Beren, Chuck Blitz, Jennifer Bloomfield, Wes Boyd, Noah Brand, Stewart Brand, Meg Brookman, Jin Chen, Napier Collyns, Joanne Conger, Elisa Cooper, Stephen Dubner, Nan Dunne, Esther Dyson, Fabrice Florin, Adam Fuller, Benjamin Fuller, John Fuller, Karen Fuller, Stephen Fuller, Pamela Gerloff, Mark Gerzon, Sharon Goldinger, Linne Gravestock, Jay Greenberg, Wade Greene, Ruth Gruber, Eileen Hammer, Stephanie Heuer, Noel Hinners, John Hobbs, David Hoffman, Tony Husch, Mary Johnson, Jo Ellen Green Kaiser, Art Kleiner, Jennifer Ladd, David Landau, Evelin Gerda Lindner, Laura Lowe, Christoph Maier, Bob Mazer, Evelyn Messinger, Tish Morgan, Barbara Morris, Morgan Moss, Jay Oglivy, Maureen O'Hara, Penny Patton, Ryan Phelan, Jennifer Prost, Thomas Purvis, Ann Richardson, Mary Lou Richardson, Peter Richardson, Suze Rutherford, Linda Seabright, Mark Sommer, Kim Spencer, Jennifer Spoerri, Ian Stonington, Ron Suny, Bill Ury, George Vamos, John Vasconcellos, and Rosalind Wiseman. I thank them all.

I also wish to thank Melanie Hart, who designed and maintains the Web site breakingranks.net, and my colleague Michael Toms, host of New Dimensions Radio, for directing me to Berrett-Koehler Publishers. The collegial interest of their professionals in what's between the covers of the books they publish is an author's dream. My special thanks to publisher Steven Piersanti for instantly grasping the book's central ideas, managing editor Jeevan Sivasubramaniam for his heartfelt support, editorial director Johanna Vondeling for her wise counsel regarding the organization and tone of the book, and Sandra Beris for her painstaking line edit.

For decades, a uniquely gifted editor has worked with me to clarify my writing. Ina Cooper began urging me to write twenty-five years ago and has edited almost everything I've done. Her work on this book and its predecessor greatly enhanced their accessibility and cogency, and I am deeply grateful.

Heartfelt thanks also to John Steiner for his inspired networking, his big-picture editorial suggestions, and his steady encouragement over the many years that this work has been in gestation.

No one has done more to strengthen the analysis of rankism than Peter Sharp, whom I have never met, but with whom I've exchanged hundreds of pages of e-mails. His incisive critique of *Somebodies and Nobodies* and his many constructive suggestions on this book have greatly sharpened the presentation. I used to puzzle over Gertrude Stein's remark that she writes for strangers. Now I understand.

My views on values, politics, and religion took shape during many conversations and a decade-long correspondence with Peter A. Putnam, a fellow graduate student at Princeton University.[1] Both of us were privileged to experience a priceless apprenticeship with John A. Wheeler, who, as mentor to generations of physicists, unstintingly went beyond the expected to share his unique style of model building with his students. Had I not been among them, I doubt this book would exist.

All Rise is dedicated to my wife, Claire Sheridan. I cannot imagine this endeavor reaching fruition without her constancy, integrity, and dignity.

Index

About the Author

ROBERT W. FULLER earned his Ph.D. in physics at Princeton University and taught at Columbia, where he coauthored the classic text *Mathematics of Classical and Quantum Physics*. The mounting social unrest of the 1960s drew his attention to educational reform, and at the age of thirty-three he was appointed president of Oberlin College, his alma mater.

In 1971 Fuller traveled to India as a consultant to Indira Gandhi, and there witnessed firsthand the famine resulting from the war with Pakistan over what became Bangladesh. With the election of Jimmy Carter, Fuller began a campaign to persuade the new president to end world hunger. His meeting with Carter in the Oval Office in June 1977 contributed to the establishment of the Presidential Commission on World Hunger.

During the 1980s Fuller traveled frequently to the USSR, working as a citizen-scientist to improve the cold war relationship. His work, together with that of others, led to the creation of the nonprofit global corporation Internews, which promotes democracy via free and independent media. For many years Fuller served as its chairman.

When the USSR collapsed, Fuller's work as a citizen-diplomat came to a close and he looked back reflectively on his career. He came to see that he had been, at different junctures in his life, both a somebody and a nobody. Contemplating his periodic sojourns into "Nobodyland" led him to identify and probe *rankism*—defined by him as abuse of the power inherent in rank—and ultimately to write *Somebodies and Nobodies: Overcoming the Abuse of Rank* (New Society Publishers, 2003). Growing popular interest in this subject led him to write the present sequel.

About Berrett-Koehler Publishers

BERRETT-KOEHLER is an independent publisher dedicated to an ambitious mission: Creating a World that Works for All.

We believe that to truly create a better world, action is needed at all levels —individual, organizational, and societal. At the individual level, our publications help people align their lives with their values and with their aspirations for a better world. At the organizational level, our publications promote progressive leadership and management practices, socially responsible approaches to business, and humane and effective organizations. At the societal level, our publications advance social and economic justice, shared prosperity, sustainability, and new solutions to national and global issues.

A major theme of our publications is "Opening Up New Space." They challenge conventional thinking, introduce new ideas, and foster positive change. Their common quest is changing the underlying beliefs, mindsets, and structures that keep generating the same cycles of problems, no matter who our leaders are or what improvement programs we adopt.

We strive to practice what we preach—to operate our publishing company in line with the ideas in our books. At the core of our approach is stewardship, which we define as a deep sense of responsibility to administer the company for the benefit of all of our "stakeholder" groups: authors, customers, employees, investors, service providers, and the communities and environment around us.

We are grateful to the thousands of readers, authors, and other friends of the company who consider themselves to be part of the "BK Community." We hope that you, too, will join us in our mission.

A BK Currents Book

This book is part of our BK Currents series. BK Currents books advance social and economic justice by exploring the critical intersections between business and society. Offering a unique combination of thoughtful analysis and progressive alternatives, BK Currents books promote positive change at the national and global levels. To find out more, visit www.bkcurrents.com.

Be Connected

Visit Our Website
Go to www.bkconnection.com to read exclusive previews and excerpts of new books, find detailed information on all Berrett-Koehler titles and authors, browse subject-area libraries of books, and get special discounts.

Subscribe to Our Free E-Newsletter
Be the first to hear about new publications, special discount offers, exclusive articles, news about bestsellers, and more! Get on the list for our free e-newsletter by going to www.bkconnection.com.

Participate in the Discussion
To see what others are saying about our books and post your own thoughts, check out our blogs at www.bkblogs.com.

Get Quantity Discounts
Berrett-Koehler books are available at quantity discounts for orders of ten or more copies. Please call us toll-free at (800) 929-2929 or email us at bkp.orders@ aidcvt.com.

Host a Reading Group
For tips on how to form and carry on a book reading group in your workplace or community, see our website at www.bkconnection.com.

Join the BK Community
Thousands of readers of our books have become part of the "BK Community" by participating in events featuring our authors, reviewing draft manuscripts of forthcoming books, spreading the word about their favorite books, and supporting our publishing program in other ways. If you would like to join the BK Community, please contact us at bkcommunity@bkpub.com.